From Wilder Shores

THE TABLES OF MY TRAVELS

From Wilder Shores

THE TABLES OF MY TRAVELS

Lesley Blanch

for Billy,
for darling Billy –
with love
Lesley
July '89

JOHN MURRAY

First published 1989
by John Murray (Publishers) Ltd
50 Albemarle Street, London W1X 4BD

British Library Cataloguing in Publication Data
Blanch, Lesley
From wilder shores.
1. Food: Regional dishes – Recipes   2.
World. Description & travel, history
I. Title
641.59

ISBN 0–7195–4692–3

Typeset, printed and bound in Great Britain by
Butler & Tanner Ltd, Frome and London

I dedicate this book to my Digestion
which has nobly supported so many surprises,
trials and unwise indulgences
throughout our long years of travel together.

Contents

Illustrations

(between pages 84 and 85)

1. The stairway at Carlton House by C. Wild
2. Tea at an Afghan *tchai-khana*, photograph by Roland and Sabrina Michaud
3. Squirrels in Sumatra
4. Merchant wife at tea by Boris Kustodiev
5. The midday meal, Cairo, by John Frederick Lewis
6. A Turkish *lokanta*
7. The coffee hearth, photograph by Nik Wheeler
8. The author's ideal Christmas dinner table

The author and publishers wish to thank the following for permission to reproduce illustrations:

Plate 1, Windsor Castle, Royal Library, © Her Majesty the Queen; Plate 2, Roland and Sabrina Michaud, and the John Hillelson Agency, London; Plate 3, The British Library; Plate 4, The Russian State Museum, Leningrad; Plate 5, The Owen Edgar Gallery, London; Plate 7, Nik Wheeler.

Acknowledgements

I wish to thank some of those friends who have been especially helpful and encouraging during the preparation of this book. For obtaining certain illustrations I thank Princess Nina Lobanov-Rostovsky, Patricia, Countess Jellicoe, and Mr Nabil Saidi. The interest and practical advice of Mr George Bradford have been as sustaining as the dishes he himself cooks with such éclat. I must also thank Madame Susan Train in Paris and Mademoiselle Yvonne Molinari in Ventimiglia; the former for her enthusiasm for my subject and the latter for bringing typed order out of chaos from my long-hand manuscript.

L.B.

NOTE

Some of these pieces have appeared (not entirely in their present form) in various American magazines during the last twelve years: 'Breakfast is best' and 'Village inventions' in *Food and Wine*, 'The wilder shores of picnicking' and 'My kind of Christmas dinner' in *House and Garden*, 'Afghanistan remembered' and 'Nile-side meals' in *Gourmet*.

Foreword

My book is not a cookery book in the classical sense, and no more than glancingly autobiographical. Nor is it strictly a travel book, although it does tell something of far lands and the circumstances which have led me to eat local dishes in a variety of local settings, from Rothschild dinner tables to Turcoman tents.

Perhaps it could be best described as a sketch book: sketches offering the dishes, places and people I have encountered while on the move through life. Do not look here, oh pedant, for precise lists of ingredients, oven temperatures or weights and measures. At least not all the time. These pages are not devised for beginners in the kitchen, nor yet for experts. Rather, they are for those who fiddle around, have had a little basic experience, enjoy experimenting and contriving imaginative extras, and generally enjoy cooking as much as eating and travelling.

Some of these pages were written in a mood of acute nostalgia, at a time when, enduring a smashed knee, I thought I would be permanently immobilised, and debarred both from the sort of journeys to distant lands that I once enjoyed, and from the foods I discovered there. Dishes kind friends prepared for me did not still my hunger. If I could not get to the place, could I not, at least, recapture the rapture of some faraway plate? But even when later I contrived to sidle my wheelchair alongside the stove to cook a version of, say, *shesteranga*, I was still overcome by ungratified desires. Thus, in psychologists' jargon, I began to write out my fantasies of place and plate – the wilder shores of cooking.

When, thirty years ago, I wrote *The Wilder Shores of Love*, my title coined a phrase which I still see scattered through the columns of the daily press: 'The Wilder Shores of Westminster', may head a piece on stormy politics; or it is The Wilder Shores of high fashion, gardening and all else, and dyspeptic friends often refer to my cooking, or menus, as being 'very Wilder Shores'. Which is as maybe.

While I sometimes indulge my readers with precise instructions, I assume that they know enough to be intrigued by a recipe given in more or less narrative or descriptive form. Which reminds me that in my first cookery book, *Round the World in Eighty Dishes*, a printer's error (or was it mine?) over the quantity of cayenne pepper to be used caused several exacerbated readers to write threatening letters, so damaging had been the measure they had blindly followed. After which I think it wiser to leave as much as possible to the reader's intuition. Recipes, which are to be found in Part Two, are generally for four unless common sense dictates otherwise. As I have said earlier, this is a book for experimenting . . .

While trying to obtain recipes of exactitude myself, I have often been stuck with a phrase which recurred with fatal frequency, in many languages. The more remote the area, the more frenzied the gestures of explanation and the fewer the precisions, but the same triumphant phrase always sounded . . . 'Then cook till *delicious*!' After all, it really says everything, and so becomes the keynote of this book. May it give you ideas, outlines and echoes of delicious faraway feasts on Wilder Shores. To you, to fill in the picture in your own way.

Part One

CHAPTER 1

Breakfast is Best

Breakfast can be the best of all meals, or the worst. It all depends on the state of your liver. It is my favourite meal – but then I have been blessed with a good liver, which has stood up to punishment, for my many journeys in remote areas must have tried it sadly. Liver and I have weathered some rough breakfasts in our time: cold plum pudding and flat champagne the day after Christmas; black-buffalo milk and onions in a Bulgarian monastery, *saucisses de Toulouse* and glasses of white wine at rather shady bars at Marseille . . . and so on, but not *ad nauseam* to me, fortunately. They say there is an attraction in opposites, and in my romantic youth, and through nerve-wracking marriages, I always seemed to be waking up beside leaden, liverish lovers. This was not the way to enjoy breakfast together. And indeed, if you cannot meet up with a liver which matches your own, it is better to breakfast alone. As for breakfasts eaten in restaurants, or in the company of several other persons, they are, I think, intolerable. This is a meal to be shared with the loved one or enjoyed alone with Darling Self, with no pressures or conversation, still less with children about, smashing at unsightly breakfast foods that are advertised to snap, crackle or crunch.

In my childhood, I was strictly relegated to my own room for whatever I ate at that time – I can't call it to mind, but I read voraciously during the meal. My mother took her china tea and toast in bed, reading *The Times*, the *Koran*, or Beatrix Potter's stories about animal families, Tom Kitten or Jeremy Fisher. She had catholic tastes. My father, almost a professional pessimist, breakfasted off very strong black coffee which he brewed himself, and a handful of nuts. He read Defoe's *Journal of the Plague Year* over and over again, for he said descriptions of such horrors made life and the daily news seem more bearable.

During the nineteenth century, breakfasts assumed a special social status, and required both stamina and notable conversational ability. I seem to remember reading that the redoubtable Margot Asquith, when a sharp-witted débutante, and a member of that eclectic group known as the Souls, was sometimes invited to the breakfasts given by Dr Jowett at Oxford, where the finest intellects of the University and political world met over sustaining fare. The literary world of mid-Victorian London also found breakfast meetings to their liking. Dickens, Carlyle and Robert Browning, like Byron and Lord Melbourne before them, were ready to talk and eat together in the morning. Though not at a really early hour: such breakfasts were usually around eleven o'clock, and might be said to resemble those brunches so popular in the States today. We must suppose that Lord Byron braced himself with his customary glass of vinegar before setting out, much as some people are brought-to by a cup of early morning tea.

Queen Victoria made a habit of breakfasting out of doors, and in her old age was photographed at Osborne, a solid black-clad figure seated on the lawn, wearing an unbecoming straw hat and further shaded by a tent under the then fashionable monkey-puzzle trees. She was flanked by her turbanned Indian servants and layer upon layer of Royal relatives, frilly little future Emperors, and wooden-looking daughters in strict boaters, almost indistinguishable from the nannies. Sometimes harassed Ministers of State would be obliged to catch a train at dawn to bring the red leather royal dispatch boxes to the breakfast table, for the Queen rose early and was soon pushing aside the plates for graver issues. At these breakfasts, one of the frilly grandchildren, who later became Queen Marie of Romania, tells us in her memoirs she used to long passionately for a special kind of brown biscuit which came from Germany in flat round tins, and which the old Sovereign loved especially. Perhaps they held memories of the adored, ever-mourned Prince Consort and so helped her to face the day of work and widowhood ahead.

In the England of my youth which, I hasten to add, was not Victorian, nor even Edwardian, I used to stay in country houses where breakfasts would have been indeed worth getting up for, were it not for the numbers of rather hearty guests assembled in the dining room. These country house-party breakfasts were in the nature of gargantuan feasts, for exercise, in one form or another, hunting, shooting or fishing, or the walks undertaken constantly by all but myself required a good, solid send-off. And that they certainly were.

Let me recall some of those spreads. A central table was laid ceremoniously; a large fire blazed – for I do not recall ever having been to such house-parties in summer – and a butler hovered beside the long sideboards – two, certainly, dominated by impressive silver or silver-gilt tea and coffee urns. Around them, in silver chafing dishes, were a variety of hot foods which were instantly replenished if they showed signs of cooling. Bacon and eggs; eggs scrambled, eggs poached, and a whole legion of soft-boiled eggs under little cosies; omelettes; smoked haddock; kedgeree; grilled kidneys and tomatoes; devilled kidneys; mushrooms; sausages; fish cakes; kippers; and cold temptations such as York ham, tongue, or cold game pie. Then there were all the breads, toasts, scones, and 'Oxford' marmalade. ... I don't remember ever seeing fruit at these feasts. But I must not omit porridge, which was the corner-stone. Porridge can be a most repulsive substance unless cooked and eaten correctly, in the Scots manner, which it always was in those far-off days, being made with a pinch of salt, and thick cream added to your fancy.

Apropos of both kedgeree and porridge, I recall a chilling anecdote which included both these dishes. In India, while an English family were enjoying their breakfast kedgeree, the youngest child wandered away into the garden with his porridge bowl. He had taken to doing this lately, and curious, his parents followed him quietly. They found him seated on a stone, beside him a king cobra, reared-up and swaying, the child feeding it spoonfuls of porridge – one for himself, one for the snake, in alternate mouthfuls. If the cobra tried for its mouthful out of turn, the child said 'Naughty!' and whacked it with the spoon, at which it drew back, obediently. ... That's a true story I sometimes think of to lighten the monotony of stirring the porridge.

Another of my pastimes, when preparing tediously long dishes, is remembering a crude jest I was once party to at a country inn in England. There, commercial travellers passing through were in the habit of leaving instructions with the night porter as to the time they wished to be called, and what they wanted for breakfast. Thus: *Room 4. Call at 8. Bacon and eggs, coffee.* Such information the night porter chalked up on a blackboard, so that when he went off duty, the kitchen staff, arriving very early, were in command of the situation. By stealing down before daylight, we succeeded in changing these orders. When the kitchen staff arrived they were surprised to see such demands as: *Room 18. Call at 6. Crème de menthe and oxtail soup ... Room 10. Call at 7. Jellied eels for 2. Rum punch.* Well, I still enjoy the joke, even if it wasn't the commercial traveller's ideal breakfast.

Now my mind turns to quite another kind – the romantic kind all loving couples have known, often in some old-fashioned sleazy Paris hotel in the *quartier latin*. Those stuffy rooms were always papered over with wild patterns of flowers and ribbons which smothered the ceilings and doors too, so that one seemed to be inside some flowery hat-box. Breakfast was brought by the *valet de chambre*, who wore a yellow and black wasp-striped waistcoat, and offered up the tray with an air of pious concentration, as if laying it on an altar – which is, after all, how the French nation regards the bed. There was *café au lait* or frothy chocolate in a very thick china jug, and the *croissants* had warm, gooey centres, and spread a flutter of golden flakes over the unyielding shiny surface of the eiderdown. After which the remains of the feast were placed outside the door, a ritual which signified one was not to be disturbed for the rest of the morning. ... Such old-fashioned hotels never had telephones by the bed to shrill tactlessly, and one I recall fondly had a bath set in an alcove almost at the bed-side, so that one rolled from one into the other, or reached out from clouds of steam for a last cup of coffee. Breakfast-in-bath is very luxurious. I have tried to recapture that rapture by taking a teapot into my bathroom, and placing it before me, on a tray across the bath. But it is not at all the same thing. Perhaps I miss the brown hand that used to pass me that extra cup of coffee. ... As I remarked earlier, breakfast can be a most romantic meal.

A picturesque one, too, as in the burning blue mornings of Tunis where I would make for the narrow streets of the medina, or Arab town, and near the twisted green and scarlet pillars of the ancient slave market, eat *brique*, a triangle of flaky pastry which imprisons a rather runny egg. Very difficult to eat neatly, I found, for there were no napkins provided, and one stood beside a little blue-tiled recess in the wall, where the *brique* vendor crouched, fanning a toy-like stove from which he conjured these delicacies. A glass of sweet green tea offered by another street vendor completed my Tunisian breakfasts.

Since I am *matinale* by nature, and like to go out to meet the morning's freshness wherever the climate allows it, in my garden, on a city roof-top terrace, ship's deck, or anywhere for that matter where I can catch the day before the rest of the world, I particularly enjoyed certain al fresco breakfasts I knew in Turkey. From the European side of the Bosphorus I used to take a very early morning ferry boat over to the Asiatic side, watching the first slanted sun's rays gilding the great mosques, or following a line of bright-painted fishing boats chugging briskly towards the Black Sea for the day's catch. While the ferry crossed over there was time to take a tiny cup of thick black coffee from an energetic boy who rushed up and down the boat balancing the cups on a swinging brass tray. Today, the Bosphorus is bridged, traffic speeds across, and there are no cups of coffee on the way.

On landing, I would take a bone-breaking little carriage and jog inland to reach a vine-wreathed yellow house overlooking one of those quiet, cypress-shaded graveyards that abound in Turkey, and are never melancholy as in the West. There, in a garden full of roses, where some old headstones topped with carved turbans had overflowed their original terrain, I would find a truly Turkish breakfast awaiting me, along with my Turcoman host. (Turcomen are not Turks, but come from the Turcoman steppes of Central Asia.) The samovar hummed in readiness, a teapot aloft, ready to offer small glasses of Caravan Tea. (Was it really such, I wonder? I liked to think it lived up to its reputation, and was brought from China, by camel-caravan.) There was fruit on that breakfast table: pomegranates, figs and grapes, and some delicious small un-named berries; but what I most enjoyed was a mixture of exceedingly rich, clotted cream made from buffalo milk, eaten with wild honey, which came from the Turkish–Iranian country bordering Azerbaijan. I think it was called *sashir*, but I doubt it could be duplicated successfully without the water buffalo's contribution: even the thickest clotted Devonshire cream would not be quite right. Ah! those breakfasts in Asia!

Some of the oddest breakfasts I ever ate were at Palm Springs, the lush playground of Hollywood's rich and famous. Each morning, as I emerged into the blinding Arizona sunlight I encountered a fellow guest, an aged figure, being wheeled out by a young and pretty nurse – a failed starlet, I later discovered. She would settle her charge under the palms where a stout breakfast awaited him. This was no less a legend than Joe Schenck, the emigré Russian boy who became president of United Artists, and later, Twentieth-Century Fox, who was responsible for the earliest Buster Keaton pictures, and the last of D. W. Griffiths' epics. In short, one of the founders of the film industry. Also, once the husband of Norma Talmadge (one of the three Talmadge sisters), a creature of such dark romantic beauty that by 1916 she reigned supreme in Hollywood.

Those early days have always fascinated me, and I used to wheedle the old mogul to talk of his life when 'Hollywood and Vine' were just two tracks crossing among the orchards; when Doug and Mary and Charlie were making movies in an old barn and the Mark Sennet bathing beauties were romping on the beach at Santa Monica; when William S. Hart and Tom Mix were galloping to the rescue of Mary Miles Minter across scrub land now the high-rise heart of down-town Los Angeles. ... A whole chimera of legend seemed to shimmer round the old survivor's wheel-chair.

'Why d'you want to know all that crap?' Mr Schenck would ask, while insisting that I shared his breakfast. As his ancient wrinkled neck emerged from the folds of his dressing-gown and his small leathery grey face turned slowly towards me, he seemed like some centuries-old tortoise. But his frail diamond-ringed hands were remarkably agile spearing bits of fried liver – his customary break-fast – and forcing them on me.

Mouthful by mouthful I downed these unwelcome tit-bits. They were the price of some unique memories. Alas! I had no tape recorder then.

Breakfasts in America seldom charmed me, but then I never reached the hush-puppies and corn-meal bread of the deep South. Driving across country to the west coast, and sleeping in motels *en route*, I found I had to go out to the nearest drug store for a lamentably weak brew of coffee, too-soft white bread and eggs 'sunny-side up'. The drug store or drive-in I encountered then lacked the allure or exoticism of my Asiatic breakfasts, in spite of the most cinematic cowboys lounging in and out. When I lived in New York, I used to see from my window the scuttling rush of city workers making for the high counter of a drug store, bolting their breakfasts standing, on their way to the office, and I did not wonder at the number of advertisements for indigestion cures which surrounded them in those same drug stores. I have always thought it unfortunate to mix meals and medicine: to eat on premises which are also a chemist's shop may be convenient – snatching another bismuth tablet as you pay the bill – but it cannot be conducive to the proper enjoyment of breakfast. Speed should have no place in either the preparation, or the eating of food. That is why it is so well worthwhile to wake up an hour earlier, and cook breakfast at home. You do not have a kitchen? But surely you have a gas ring, or an electric kettle? Surely you can make tea or coffee, and enjoy what might be ambiguously described as a Roll in bed with Honey?

But stop! Have I seemed harsh about American breakfasts? How could I? Some can be among the best in the world, and I remember fondly those I used to enjoy when I lived in Hollywood. For them, I did not grudge the getting up, the going out – as it were, breakfast on the hoof. I was then writing *The Sabres of Paradise*, and sometimes began around three in the morning, so that by six I was mad with hunger, and tempted by the loveliness of dawn over the California hills. Then I would head for a drive-in called Norm's (my adored cat was called Norman which made it seem even nicer). There, before eight o'clock, you could eat as much as you liked for under a dollar – and with very amusing company too: husky truck-drivers, and straying starlets, their false eyelashes awash with tears of self-pity as they told how they hadn't got the part promised the night before. ... Strange company, so full of friendliness over the eggs 'sunny-side up', the delicious hash-brown potatoes with fried bacon and syrup-drenched waffles. ... Such were the fulfilments by dawn's early light.

Now while some of the foregoing food might appear too enflaming for a sultry summer morning, I suggest an unlikely alternative, something that helped me, long ago, to survive August in a New York apartment without air-conditioning. Cucumber sandwiches, which I cut wafer-thin *the night before*, were wrapped in a slightly dampened cloth.* That was the technique of those lofty English butlers who once ruled below stairs, and to whom by tradition, the making of this particular sandwich was entrusted. No doubt they were designed specifically for tea-time and not made long ahead. Great country houses of the past were nothing if not conventional

---

*Be sure to take your sandwiches out of the cloth half an hour or so before eating them, or they remain too damp.

and tea-time was a sacred ritual, observed punctiliously: plum cake and crumpets in winter, beside the fire, and cucumber sandwiches and caraway seed cake in summer, on the lawn. But I remember my own cucumber sandwiches, accompanied by iced coffee, successfully soothing the most fretful dawns.

The planning of what we eat, at what hour, should not be rigid.

CHAPTER 2

Afghanistan Remembered

Although these pages set out to be predominantly on food and local cuisine, it is almost impossible to write of the peaceful country I knew and the Afghan dishes I savoured there when I must recall it today, across barriers of bloodshed and privation. Thus, anything I write here must be taken as a valedictory gesture, hailing the Afghanistan I once knew.

There was still a king in Kabul when first I went there, but his was an austere majesty, with few trappings, and a preoccupation with agricultural development and model farms before palace life. It was among the tribes, such as the Kuchi, that one glimpsed a certain intoxicating glitter composed of coin jewellery, babies tricked out in *kincob*, a sort of gold tissue fabric splashed with bouquets of impossible flowers, their skull-caps gold-embroidered or sewn with pearls and coral beads. As to the cavaliers – they were mud-splashed or dusty, but sumptuous, with velvet saddle-cloths, and guns studded with turquoise – a strangely foppish crew, their eyes heavily rimmed with kohl, their turbans rakishly tipped. The women, glimpsed in the tents, were spangled in sequinned veils with a jangling mass of heavy silver ornaments, one and all exotic creatures to find amid the barren wastes. They swarmed down from their rocky fastnesses and enticed us into their encampments to share a stew of goats' meat or wild partridge while their huge angry dogs circled round the cauldrons. Among the Kuchi, I sampled *dugh*, a beverage of watered-down yoghourt perfumed with mint – a change from the usual brew of sweet green tea.

The Afghans, a people who are said to be both genial and cruel, according to their mood, always showed me their genial side. So welcoming were they that every encounter, every meal or casual roadside halt appeared a festive occasion. From the come-by-chance meetings to the hospitality of friends of friends, the garage hands, shepherds, merry marriage parties dancing and singing as they escorted the bride's camel, or the lorry drivers and their beguiling *batcha* boys – all made me welcome with an air of swaggering gallantry.

These *batcha* boys are an essential part of the Asiatic scene: pleasure-boys, they were called, in Samarkand, where once they danced for the Emirs and became petted favourites. ('A woman for breeding, a boy for pleasure' runs the Asiatic saying.) The Afghan *batcha* boys I saw had little time for languorous undulations – they accompanied the lorries, rushed to place a big stone under the back wheels when the brakes gave up on a mountain road, and went about the *tchai-khanas*, preparing sustenance for their drivers before performing any further unspecified duties required of them.

I came to observe that the more handsome the *batcha* boy, the longer the noon-day halt and the more the driver emerged rested and refreshed from the shadowed depths of the *tchai-khana*. Thus I took to selecting a lorry with what my nanny used to describe as 'a likely looking lad' aboard, which ensured I should not be hurried along the way, torn from congenial surroundings such as a *tchai-khana* where rug-merchants gathered. In padded caftans they crouched beside their dark crimson rugs, the 'royal' bokharas (whose traditional octagonal medallion design is said to represent an elephant footprint) and engaged me, language problems or no, in flowery exchanges, pressing me to endless glasses of mint tea. And was it commerce alone that made them so delightfully hospitable? Rather, Afghan geniality.

Recalling such encounters a yearning – almost a home-sickness – seizes me for I loved Afghanistan passionately. A kaleidoscope of scenes rises around me as I stand in my Western kitchen trying to prolong Afghan emotions by making *bouloni*. This is a kind of wheaten cake stuffed with green-vegetable tops. My driver's two mothers (his father enjoying the Moslem plural) prepared this for me with loving hospitality, one of a dozen or more delights, when I visited the family in their rickety balconied dwelling high above the warrens of Kabul's Shor bazaar. . . . They made the same *bouloni* again, for that sad but hilarious farewell party they offered me at Jalalabad, their winter quarters (for Kabul's winter temperatures are unimaginably severe). It was there I spent my last hours on Afghan soil . . . Jalalabad . . . a name now written in crimson for the blood shed in that frontier region.

A saucepan boils over, and I am whirled back through time and space to my own kitchen surrounded by stainless steel gadgets, mixers, whisks, a refrigerator and running hot and cold water. How can I hope my *bouloni* will taste like theirs? Or that any other of the dishes I ate amid those wild hills could be reproduced here? Yet the spell is potent. I turn away from the electric chop-slice-grind-machine, and slide back into the dream. I am once more in a large caravanserai, or wayside halt, near Ghazni. Fumes of cooking, a gigantic samovar puffing steam, and rows of bright painted teapots (as all over Central Asia, it is customary to offer one to each customer). There is a clatter and roar of gaudily painted lorries drawing up, and the turbanned drivers swagger in to command attention. . . . Now I am airing my few phrases of Pushtu, exchanging a packet of biscuits ('Assorted Hostess') for some mulberries dried to form a sort of paste. I try to say how sad I am to be leaving next day, at which a *beaux ténébreux* who is nibbling a biscuit appreciatively, while looking fierce enough to devour a tiger, flashes his kohl-rimmed eyes (here, the dandies favour a plum-red kohl in place of the usual sooty grey) and presents me with his snuff box.

All Afghan men carried such boxes, little gourds, polished, and mounted in rough silver, to hold *naswr*, an explosive greenish powder often their sole luxury. The gourds were topped by a shaving-brush-like tuft of horse-hair, by which the snuff-taker brushed away any traces of the powder which might remain. This elegant, curiously sophisticated gesture always reminded me of the manner in which even the most virile Spanish men use their fans, flicking them open or shut, in a sort of personal pronouncement, or signature, of elegance.

I have treasured my gourd-gift through many years, as I treasure every memory of the Afghanistan I knew – once upon a time, a happy, happy time, long ago and far away ... now as far away, it seems, as peace, in that tormented land. But, as this is no place for politics, allow me a historical digression.

It has always been customary to imagine Afghanistan as a remote, dour scene, a savage land inhabited by fierce tribes only. The tribesmen – called moujaheddin today – are still there, as much part of the land as those cut-throat gorges such as the Khourd Kabul Pass, even more wild than the Khyber of Kiplingesque legend. (It was in the dark defiles of the Khourd Kabul Pass that the British army of occupation was wiped out in 1842.) Yet behind all the fury and cruelty of such scenes there was, historically, a brilliant setting which requires some effort of imagination. The Afghans understood luxury – in their own manner: many had superb weapons and horses, while fine carpets, priceless cashmere shawls, and elephants, jewelled and majestic, were part of that Kabul life which centred round the amirs and khans. One of these, Shah Shuja, possessed the fabled Koh-i-noor diamond and wore it in his turban, from where it moved first to the sleeve of Ranjit Singh, the Sikh ruler, and finally to the crown of England.

But then, Central Asia *is* extravagant, dramatic and fierce, and the savage pride of their Mongol, Turcoman and Affridi forebears became an Afghan characteristic. That is something successive waves of invaders have, over the centuries, learned to their cost.

It is, too, something that can be traced in the Afghan cuisine, extravagant and unpredictable, as varied and coloured as the land itself. From the bleak Turcoman steppes touching Iran to the lush groves round Kandahar, nudging Pakistan, there is great virility in the dishes. Though less sophisticated than Iranian, Turkish or Arabic, Afghan food has its own subtleties. I recall many coloured and spiced rice dishes: *norange*, for example, was rice tinted with orange rind and pimento; while *zamrod*, or emerald, cast a spinachy glow, and dried and powdered grapes were used to impart a violet bloom to grilled meat. *Kebabs*, grilled chunks of meat, attain true perfection here, even at the roughest wayside halt, beneath those giant plane trees that Tamerlane's Golden Horde are said to have first planted. My enthusiasm for Afghan food should not be attributed to any alcoholic haze, for wine is seldom found in Moslem lands, the general Afghani beverage being tea, green or black, flavoured with mint or cardamom, while there is also garlic tea, or a rose-leaf brew, for the more fanciful.

It is by the range of *kebabs* that the Afghan cuisine comes into its own. In the capital – unlovely, yet fascinating Kabul – even in the most humble restaurants (there were few stylish ones) *kebabs* were an unfailing pleasure. Along the wildest tracks, or by some village coppersmith's booth, the same excellence prevailed. I recall in particular those eaten in the dramatic setting of the bazaar at Tash-Kurgan, in the north, near the river Oxus, which remains almost unchanged since Marco Polo passed that way. There the low, vaulted ceilings are made flowery by innumerable ancient Chinese plates and saucers plastered into the surface – rare pieces, I fancy, though unrecognised as such for they are casualties of the age-old caravans that followed the Silk Route from Cathay through Tash-Kurgan towards the west. But back to the *kebabs* we ate from tin plates – adieu the celestial porcelain.

There are many kebabs, each originating in a different province. *Pushtu kebab*, from the north-east, has morsels of meat (always lamb) first marinated in yoghourt (or *mast* as it is called there). The meat is then poached lightly, before being grilled fast. Thus tenderised, the succulent morsels almost swoon off the skewer. *Lulu kebab* is little sausagey pieces of minced meat and garlic. Best of all, *khorak* or *kebabi i sihri*. Here, small chunks of meat alternate with pieces of fat grilled crisply brown. A preponderance of fatty bits on one's skewer is considered the *bonne bouche*, expressing the cook's regard. Or so I have been told. In any case, as I relished both fat and lean, waves of mutual appreciation wafted between the cook, in his lean-to kitchen, and myself, cross-legged and cramped before a rickety mouse-high table on the verandah which served as dining-room beside the roads I long to travel once more.

Afghan melons and grapes were always legendary throughout Central Asia. The Emperor Babur, who adored Afghanistan and chose to lay his bones on a verdant hillside outside Kabul, was kept supplied with Afghan melons during his long years of conquest in India. Afghanistan boasts sixty varieties of grape, many of which are dried and stored against the snow-bound Afghan winters. In those long ice-bound months many families across the countryside still lived immured in grim fortress-like *qalas*, high-walled domains built round central courts. Here several generations, with their cattle, domestic animals, stored crops and fuel, were all snowed up till the release of spring. Here they lived, loved, quarrelled, gave birth or died, isolated from any contact with the outside world, for the roads over the mountains that divide the valleys are then impassable by man or beast. In happier times *aft mewa* was prepared in the late autumn months. All kinds of fruits, apricots, peaches, plums, grapes, apples, and mulberries were soaked in hot water, until softened, then mixed with chopped almonds and walnuts and left to dry, finally becoming a sort of sticky cake reserved for specially festive occasions.

It is the mulberry which provides the most value, nutritionally.

The Afghans always took bars of this fruit, dried, to sustain them on the road. Now, probably, it sustains them in battle.

Seshtaranga was to me the most exotic of all Afghan dishes. In fact it is simply composed of eggs laid on a purée of onions, vinegar and sugar added. It would make a splendid emergency luncheon dish with which to puzzle, or dazzle unexpected guests. It was very popular among the Ismaili Moslems, for their sect allows them vinegar which, being a derivation of wine, is theoretically denied the strict Sunni Moslems, and quite out of the question for the even stricter Shiite brethren. Sunnis are the majority in Afghanistan, and I have been offered *seshtaranga* at several Sunni tables, and now enjoy it at my own.

And apropos eggs. Those superb horses bred and trained for the national *bouz-kachi* game, a sort of savage polo originating in the steppes of Central Asia, were fed twenty eggs at a time (in better times no doubt) to keep up their strength. They were as pampered as our Western football heroes: I used to see them, cajoled and cossetted by their turbanned grooms, covered in padded and gaily embroidered blankets, waiting beside their riders, that formidable assembly of slit-eyed, fur-capped centaurs from Maimana and Khunduz, where the game takes the cavalcade thundering across the steppes, seven miles or more in a single run.

Where are those centaurs now? Where their brave horses? Hail and farewell.

CHAPTER 3

In Praise of Puddings

P uddings have nice names, and nice faces too, like most cakes. Yet for many years they have been elbowed aside by ices and their cousin the flamboyant sundae, or fruits which leave the waistline unthreatened. But what splendours are lost! Puddings are part of the English tradition. One hundred and sixty listed kinds can challenge the galaxy of curries and spiced dishes of the Eastern table. Puddings should be considered part of our cultural heritage, a sacred trust, for which some affiliation with the National Trust might even be envisaged.

Consider them, in all their glory. Treacle Tart, golden and crispy, Jam Tarts or Turnovers, little pastry pockets of ruby jam. Those two swarthy charmers, Chocolate Pudding and Christmas Pudding, Bread-and-Butter Pudding, Chestnut Pudding, Cabinet Pudding, Summer Pudding, Bachelor's Pudding, Guards' Pudding, Nuns' Pudding, Canary Pudding, Rice Pudding – exquisite when made with cream and brown sugar. And so it goes, working up to a voluptuous fortissimo with the classic Suet Pudding and its variations: Spotted Dick, Roly-Poly Pudding, Apple Dumplings, Treacle Hat, Apple Hat, or something to justify suet forever – Herodotus Pudding, for, yes, ancient Greece knew all about suet, mixing it with honey, figs and raisins, thus preceding the Date Pudding of my London childhood.

Looking back on those faraway days it is all the suety puddings that I remember most vividly and miss most today, living on Mediterranean shores, where, Herodotus or no, they do not seem to fit. However, they remain an outstanding treat sometimes accorded me by long-suffering friends when I visit England. ... ('She's not coming to us till Easter – but we thought a Christmas Pudding might keep her from asking for those ghastly jam roly-polys. ... What did you give her last year?' ... 'Well ... steak and kidney pudding one night, and a huge pork pie the next ... all of it suet ... I thought I'd faint, but Edward and the children adored it.')

There are, of course, a few disagreeable, or disagreeably named puddings which undermine the glowing suety whole. Old cookery books are full of such doubtful pleasures as Half-Pay Pudding (one version has carrots and mashed potato among other ingredients) or Hygienic Pudding, a mixture less forbidding than it sounds, with chestnut flour, desiccated coconut, ground walnuts and an egg or two. Tapioca Pudding remains irredeemable, a shuddering horror; Humble Pudding, like Railway Pudding does not inspire confidence. But The Good Daughter's Mincemeat Pudding, quoted in Eliza Acton's classic cookery book sounds succulent. Was it, I wonder, so named for good conduct, or did the daughter win the appellation for having invented it? On what train was Railway Pudding served? Scarcely the Orient Express. Such exotic names as The King of Oudh's Omelette arouse our interest, and here I can indulge your curiosity. The king, whose title was self-styled, started out as a mere Nawab Wazir, ruling over the dazzlingly coloured territory of Oudh, in upper India. This picturesque, dashingly moustached figure was made much of by the East India Company in the early years of the nineteenth century for he went along with their rulings and was much given to aping English ways, entertaining the sahibs and memsahibs showily. There is a primitive painting of a banquet held in his pinnacled palace beside the Gumti river where the king presides over a long table crowded round with a turbanned court. The king wears an ermine cloak and a high, tiara-like crown. He is seated between Lord and Lady Moira (whom the artist has rendered as rather squashed-looking figures). The spread is tremendous, a groaning board, although among all the dishes, bowls, epergnes, goblets and decanters it is impossible to distinguish precisely the victuals. No doubt the famous omelette was among them and some contemporary Anglo-Indian memoirs speak of a hundred eggs and terrifyingly fiery trimmings. But its legend reached early Victorian England in muted form: Eliza Acton allows it only six eggs, and later cookery books transmute it entirely to a sweet dish, with a lot of sugar, becoming a sort of jam pancake. Yet the name sticks.

Thame Tart is perhaps less well known today, but in the 1930s it lured a whole generation of undergraduates from their studies at

Oxford to a celebrated inn, the Spread Eagle, at Thame: and not only the sweet-toothed young. The Spread Eagle was celebrated for its original style, the best traditional English cooking, lovely old rooms furnished with the finest of furniture, and a splendid cellar, the whole being the creation of that most eccentric and eclectic figure, John Fothergill. But what about the Tart? Well, if I remember rightly, it was a short pastry base, upon which were piled alternate layers of raspberry jam, lemon curd, jam again and cream. Now this may sound more suited to the youthful, unsophisticated palate, yet even the most selective bibbers laid aside their wine glasses and stopped talking vintages to tuck in when Thame Tart appeared.

Christmas Pudding, which must rank as the apotheosis of all puds, was not always placed pudding-wise on the menu. At Balmoral, where in 1895 Queen Victoria was entertaining the Empress Eugénie, one of the French ladies-in-waiting was much surprised to find this pudding being served before the roast, since such was the custom for Sunday dinner parties in the Royal household, dating from the reign of George III. No doubt the Empress thought it just one more example of Britain's lack of finesse in matters gastronomic.

Indeed, this point might well be proved by *The Memsahib's Cook Book*, a tattered copy of which fell into my hands on a street stall in Delhi. It provided me with compulsive, morbid reading. Weights and measures, like coinage, are all given in Hindi. So many *tolahs* of milk, so many *attocks* of sago, and so forth. There is no mention of the King of Oudh's omelette. Some of the recipes, notably one called Flannel Rolls, lead me to agree with those historians who claim that it was indeed the memsahibs' arrival on the nineteenth-century Indian scene which was, in part, responsible for the Mutiny: the ladies' strong racial prejudices and their haughty treatment of the natives became intolerable – and indeed the type of insular, puritanical housewife reflected in such killjoy dishes as Flannel Rolls only substantiates my theory.

Let us return to the sensuous abandon of some traditional, but more prettily named English puddings. Here are a few of my favourites: Summer Pudding, Junket, Gooseberry Fool, St Leonard's Pudding and Honeycomb Cream – this last a truly summery-flummery delight. Eighteenth-century cookery books such as that of Mrs Hannah Glasse define Flummery as a sort of syllabub, sometimes adding elderflower wine to the cream. Dishes like these conjure a rustic scene, one of Gainsborough's family groups: 'the quality', seated under a spreading oak, children and dogs gambolling merrily in the foreground. It was for the likes of these that Mrs Glasse wrote her immortal pages which cover not only syllabubs and seed cake but methods of baking an ox's head, 'raising a salade in two hours by the fire' (mustard seeds in fresh horse dung), how to distil red rose-buds, or make a reserve supply of Hysterical Water – which might be the answer to all those pressures and stresses we now combat with tranquillisers.

Here, I should like to mention – to hail, rather, St Leonard's Pudding, for to me it remains all mystery, all nostalgia. Its saintly name aroused my infant curiosity, which was never gratified, for no-one I knew knew anything about the saint in question, and no more did I, even when I lived, for a brief and happy moment of my life, in one of the lovely old houses in that loveliest part of Chelsea, St Leonard's Terrace. It was war-time London, with all its restrictions, so I never obtained the required ingredients, jam, sugar, white of egg and all else. In London, then, we used a nauseous substance known as powdered egg, and sugar was only available in doll's-house proportions. Today I look round my over-stocked kitchen with a sense of wonder and thankfulness. Everything to hand – green pastures indeed. But then, as I reach for the mixing bowl I hear the Ogre Overweight snarling behind me. Best stick to sorbets.

CHAPTER 4

Meals on Wheels

The sort of wheels I have in mind are not those of trolleys carrying hot food to the needy. I am thinking, rather, of a mighty whirring and clash of steel on steel – the wheels of express trains hurtling powerfully across limitless tracks, swaying, rocking, steaming, with interminable narrow corridors down which lurching figures fight their way to the restaurant car – for better or worse.

Once, railway meals consisted of stale buns or questionable sausage rolls, obtainable *en route* from the station refreshment rooms. *Refreshment* indeed! Gloomy and grimy, Dickens immortalised them in *Mugby Junction*. Restaurant cars were comparative late-comers to rolling-stock and took time and technical know-how to achieve those standards of comfort which now seem to have declined or vanished from most lines, like the restaurants themselves. So, since we must now generally content ourselves with plastic-wrapped plastic-tasting food and coffee in plastic cups rushed along the platform just as the train moves off, we may be said to be back to square one – Mugby Junction.

Not so long ago, before jet planes began flinging their passengers from one side of the world to the other in a matter of hours, meals on wheels were taken seriously, like the comfort of the passengers. I am remembering the luxury of the Train Bleu, running between Paris and the Côte d'Azur, or the legendary Orient Express when it sped through Europe to the Sirkeci station at Istanbul. But more of these paragons later.

American friends have described nostalgically the joys of travelling on the celebrated Acheson Topeka and Santa Fe line, once a matter of three days and nights, from Chicago all across the huge continent to California. Such a journey was regarded as a kind of holiday – a rest cure even, though certainly not a slimming one for the food was superlatively good. As the train proceeded on its leisurely way various stops provided local specialities. Thus at a halt called, let us say, One Man Squaw Lakes, the chef would take aboard the freshest of trout, or the best catch of the day. Further along some southern speciality, and corn-meal mush or hush-puppies, newly baked, would grace the breakfast table. The black attendants were like family retainers, and cherished their passengers. Clothes were pressed, shoes cleaned, drinks iced to perfection, and a favourite dish or birthday cake could be ordered *en route*, so long was that *route*.

I have always relished train journeys, the longer the better, meals or no. Thus the Trans-Siberian's alleged *ennui* of endless empty steppes and appalling food was as nothing compared to the extraordinary drama of crossing from Russia in Europe to Russia in Asia and heading for China. Every mile of that vast trajectory was to me the fulfilment of a childhood's longing of which I have written elsewhere.* Those chill wastes did not seem interminable as they flowed past, often enlivened by glimpses of marmots; whole colonies of these engaging little creatures crowded out of their burrows to watch the great train pass. Perhaps they found us a diversion from monotony. People on the train waved to them with childish glee and I always expected the marmots to wave back. Along the way there were villages of small squat wooden dwellings – *izbas*, with their traditional gingerbread fretwork ornamentation (each rather dwarfed by a powerful aerial). Their little front gardens were often occupied by large wooden figures of bears, in the manner some English gardens sport gnomes. But these bear figures were practical, for they were fanciful beehives. From a navel-like hole in their middles, bees streamed in and out. When we stopped at the rare stations along the way, there were always pots of honey for sale, together with eggs and bunches of flowers. I ate a lot of honey on that journey.

Mischka the bear plays a large part in Russian folklore. There were more bears to be seen at some of the stations, now fashioned from some unknown evergreen, delightful examples of topiary skill. The creatures generally held a red flag in their twiggy paw, like some vegetal station master.

Not all the route was so playful. There were long dark hours, only cheered by continuous relays of tea from the samovars which

*__Journey into the Mind's Eye__, 1968.

boiled perpetually at the end of each corridor. Those dark hours reflected the dense forests we traversed – the Taiga of sinister repute, where wolves, Siberian tigers and starvation awaited escaping convicts (see Jules Verne's *Michel Strogoff* and other more reliable sources). Then there were stretches of desolation and destruction where some mighty river had overflowed its banks. But skirting the satiny expanses of Lake Baikal, deepest of all inland seas, they told me, everyone in the restaurant car sprang to their feet and toasted its unfathomable depths. And apropos the restaurant car, what about the meals? What, honey apart, did I eat during those five days on wheels? What did I eat? Caviar. Caviar? Yes, all the way. I turned in all my different meal tickets, renouncing round-the-clock relays of stew, fish, soup and stew again, for caviar *tout court*. Caviar, tea and black bread for breakfast; caviar, white bread and honey for luncheon, tea and more honey at tea time; caviar, vodka and toast for dinner, with Caucasian champagne, the sort Alexandre Dumas so unkindly described as epileptic cocoa. True, it was sweetish, but it was all part of the hallucinatory nature of that journey.

Two short overnight journeys where food was taken seriously, with a fervent sense of national pride, were those of the Flying Scotsman, and the Royal Highlander. The first ran from London to Edinburgh, the other, to Inverness, I think. Each must linger in the mind of anyone who can enjoy breakfast on a robust scale. That meal on those trains was all-glorious, traditional Scottish fare, reaching a fortissimo with porridge, Finnan haddock, herrings fried in oatmeal, bannocks, baps, drop scones and Dundee marmalade. To the Scots this is the food of their forebears. To others, quite simply a treat. To the uninitiated, the restaurant car's menu (tartan-edged) read rather wildly: I seem to remember as a child, spelling out Stovies, Abroath Smokies, Buttery Rowies, and asking for all of them, until repressed. The dinner menu of the night before had offered the sort of thing no child could ignore – Crowdie-Mowdie, Skink, or even once, and blazed into my memory, Rumbledethumps. There was also more recognisable fare, salmon, roast beef and chicken – concessions to outsiders, to those from South of the Border. The restaurant car was always crammed with archetypal, laird-like tweedy figures, often kilted, all eating with immense gusto. There was nothing of the 'dour' Scot about them; they were affable, but there was a faintly chauvinistic air of superiority that hedged them round. One was aware that England was a long way away: one was abroad, among foreigners: but *how* one was enjoying that foreign food.

I suppose that the acme of civilised travel and exquisite meals *en route* was once merited by the Train Bleu. Observe that I use the past tense, for its former perfection is no more. It was never extravagantly exotic like the Orient Express, but it was synonymous with unostentatious luxury and that *douceur de vivre* of which France could once boast (past tense again). Today it conforms to more utilitarian ways. The restaurant has become a bar, with snacks, and breakfast comes clattering along the corridor (if it comes at all) and consists of hunkish rolls and coffee in plastic cups. Attendants are few and far between. Comfort is cold.

The celebrated train that I am recalling left the Gare de Lyon around nine in the evening, thus allowing those who wished to, to dine first at the station's famous restaurant. There, décor, service and cuisine epitomised the elegance of *la belle époque*. Today, although still functioning in a rather diminished form, the restaurant is now classified as a national treasure. Passengers who preferred to dine later on the train found the restaurant car in a glow of pink-shaded table lamps, with perfect service and an almost sacerdotal hush awaiting them. The menu demanded such reverence. A *velouté léger au fumet de poularde et foie gras aux truffes noires* would indicate the sort of gastronomic standards then upheld by the Compagnie Internationale des Wagons-Lits. But then, passengers on this train, both before and after World War I, were a high-flying lot. Russian grand dukes and their mistresses; Egyptian princes, bankers, prima donnas, *poules de luxe*, card-sharpers thinly disguised as *hommes du monde*, ballerinas, diplomats and multi-millionaires, as well as numbers of lesser fry. The valets and maids who ministered to them were all aboard, eating, drinking, sleeping soundly, sleeping badly, or up to no good, according to circumstance. And next morning, after coffee and exquisite croissants, they each went their separate ways to the grand hotels, the casinos or villas that awaited them, while the chef and his minions set about preparing further meals for the return journey.

Another train which used to arrive periodically at Nice – though not at the station proper – and was the object of much speculation, was that owned by a Russian railway magnate. He had contrived, by a series of intricate connections, branch lines, shunting-yards and special signals, to run his private train from Moscow across Europe, via Warsaw and Vienna till, by lines laid through the park surrounding an immense turreted château he had built at Cimiez, above Nice, it steamed to a triumphant stop before his own door.

There is a barbaric, Asiatic, splendour in such a feat. I like to imagine the scene. Majestic and bearded, the millionaire emerges, snow still seeming to powder the sable collar of his greatcoat. Following him, a family procession: the *barinya*, his wife, sons, daughters, nurses, governesses, tutors, the resident doctor, maids, valets, grooms, his favourite mare, the children's pony, a pug, a couple of borzois and some of the eighty musicians engaged to play in the theatre attached to the château. Above all, a figure of primordial importance, the chef. Probably Russian by birth, he will certainly have been trained by a French master chef at Cubats, the best restaurant in St Petersburg. Thus both a French and a Russian cuisine will have been obtainable on the train. Yet however many lobsters Thermidor or *crème brulées* were served, we may be sure there were often vociferous demands for *stchee* (cabbage soup) or salted herrings, homely fare in keeping with the samovar puffing on a massive marble-and-mahogany sideboard specially designed for this magic train, as was the chef's own wagon with its lavish assembly of pots and pans, pastry boards, ice-boxes, ovens and grills.

I still recall with anguish a train journey, with meals *en route*, which I made on a trip with my husband down the west coast of Mexico, heading for Chiapas country and ultimately Guatemala. At Tehuantepec on the isthmus, the train had appeared reassuring, with a restaurant car and a lavatory (though this remained firmly locked). The menu proved to be entirely smothered in excruciatingly hot sauces, but I am not usually one to draw back from the tables of my travels so I wept my way through lunch. 'Better one's throat be lined with tin' wrote Madame Calderon de la Barca, the Scottish wife of a distinguished Mexican, when first confronted by the local cuisine.

Beyond Ixhuatan we were abruptly transferred to an open box-car, the kind used to transport railroad workers. There was, it seemed, a revolution further ahead and we waited for the sound of gunfire. Long torrid hours followed, hours of a foreboding hush, broken only by the scaly sound of claws – vultures, or zapilotes, shifting in the overhanging trees. They too were no doubt awaiting a meal on wheels – ourselves. When at last food was brought from a nearby village, they flapped off to watch malevolently from afar. This would be an unusual and rather dramatic picnic, we decided, our wretched dehydrated mouths watering as a series of pretty baskets were passed round. But the turtle eggs were rancid, *tamales* with a mush of fried ant eggs and more chillis did not tempt. Tequila is not thirst-quenching and the water seemed dubious. . . .

At the far end of the box-car a whole family of peons who were transplanting south sat wedged between their high-piled *lares et penares*, baskets, bird cages, a cradle, painted trunks and a sewing machine. An enormous squashy boa constrictor accompanied them and was dozing, wound cosily round its owner. I knew such creatures were kept as rat-catchers in many households: indeed, I had stayed, behind locked doors, in a small hotel at Tapachula where one was let loose at night and slithered about on its rounds. But box-car proximity was not relaxing, and quite spoilt my appetite for further samples of local hospitality. Even when pressed to more *tamales*, now encasing roast iguana meat decoratively arranged on banana leaves, I had no stomach for them. In Mexico, the iguana is considered a delicacy, like chicken, but now, in this lost tropic zone I remembered being told that certain Indians believe it mates with scorpions and vipers and is therefore unclean.

During those dragging hours of night I began to long passionately for the freshness of a special Mexican brew, a sickly rather nursery-like affair where strained cornmeal and sugar are whipped to a froth with chocolate and flavoured with frangipani petals. It was not forthcoming, however I pronounced its name. The villagers stared their black basilisk stare, shrugged, and padded off back to their hammocks slung between the palms. We only proceeded on our way at dawn, still fortunately without sound of gunfire. Fortunately, too, without the boa constrictor, for it and its family had transferred to a cart. Thus I was spared having to witness the reptile's being fed a breakfast of live mice – its sort of meals on wheels.

There is a mystique surrounding certain great trains; their speed, the scenery through which they pass, their luxury or cuisine adding to their legend. But the Orient Express offered further enticements.

It was as if its wagons-lits, like its restaurant and the length of its softly carpeted corridors were all enclosed in some special dimension of magic. It was an ambiance which promised romance, danger and those remote Balkan horizons where anything might happen and often did. Brigands, wolves, and halts at Ruritanian capitals while *en route* for the Turkish terminus were the stuff of adventure. The passengers, too, seemed part of the mystique, playing their roles for the duration of the run but having no being elsewhere. Darkling moustached figures in fur-lined overcoats and bearing palpably false papers came aboard and pursued ladies of dubious origin but breathless beauty. Men of business were never commercial travellers, always key figures of international finance. Children were rarely seen: if one was, then he was closely guarded and said to be heir apparent to some remote kingdom. There were regular relays of diplomats and sometimes their wives (of which, briefly I was one). The couriers, who carried the diplomatic bags or pouches to and from the various embassies were by tradition chained to their bags which made theft difficult, but visits to the lavatory or the restaurant car still more of a problem.

In such a highly-charged atmosphere, the exquisite menus on which the Compagnie Internationale des Wagons-Lits prided itself became of secondary importance. For all the chef's skill, and the *maître d'hôtel*'s suave presence, the dining car was first a hot-bed of political intrigue and romantic imbroglios. Therefore let us take on trust that the sort of menus which began with a *Fricassée de homard aux coquilles St Jacques aux pistaches* were, like the wines, all *premier cru*. Here again, I write in the past tense, for the much publicised Orient Express of today, which now does an overnight run to Venice but no further, is, for all its laboriously revived or revamped luxury, its sybaritic bedding and food, only a pale shadow of the original – a costly charade. It can never be more than that. Where, today, is that unique ambiance of mystery and intrigue – where those remarkable passengers who were once a vital part of the whole? They were larger than life, but they do not come that way any more and the Orient Express has become a ghost train.

The Orient Express which I knew, although the real thing, had only just resumed its Paris–Istanbul run at the end of World War II, and it was still a skeletal affair, with no restaurant car attached but still a lot of drama and intrigue remained. Passengers often sat up all night when the sleepers were overcrowded, and everyone brought copious picnics, often of a primitive order, to last the vagaries of a journey which might be prolonged for five or six days, snowed up or with engine trouble, or as once I recall, delayed by Yugoslav partisans, wild-looking groups then still skirmishing across undefined territories around Venezia Giulio. One of the partisan commanders, a gallant type, swaggeringly handsome in a shaggy white sheepskin jacket, took a fancy to me while examining my diplomatic passport and the numerous packages which cluttered the compartment. On his orders our train was held up for twenty-four hours (no thought about schedules then) to the mystification of the passengers and the exasperation of the old *controlleur*, who was of a conservative nature and mistrusted zones of partisan influence. Meanwhile a very merry party was organised by these warriors, who sang and danced round the fires they lit beside the track, and the commander and I toasted each other in toothmugs full of slivovitz. Even then, on so unorthodox an occasion, a mysterious element of romantic danger seemed to emanate from the train as if from some essence or eternal part of its being. ... But I cannot recall exactly what we ate.

At the Paris Exhibition of 1898, at a time when trains that served meals were for most people as much a novelty as journeys to distant lands, one enterprising restaurateur launched a pavilion which enthralled the public. Tables were placed in front of a ceaselessly unwinding panorama, giving diners the impression of rapidly changing scenes. Thus, with the hors-d'œuvres they seemed to be gliding past the Swiss Lakes, the Leaning Tower of Pisa, the bay of Naples, the Acropolis, the Bosphorus, or even further afield, mouthful by mouthful. Indian temples (not, we suppose, the burning *ghats* at Benares), Fujiyama's snowy cone, the Pyramids, Niagara Falls; the whole wonderful world of beyond reeled past, to distract them from their lobster Thermidor and subsequent delicacies. We are not told if verisimilitude went to the lengths of causing the pavilion to sway, jolt and rattle like a real dining-car.

CHAPTER 5

Village Inventions
My Roquebrune Kitchen

T here was only one shop in my village most of the year, which made housekeeping difficult – or perhaps very simple. This all-purpose grocery store sold, besides groceries, a few tinned goods, champagne (of a kind), milk and butter, and some local fruit and vegetables. There was the baker, of course, for he has always been the pivot of French village living. Once there had been a butcher, but he had gone, only lately to be replaced. Fish used to be brought up to us once a week by an old beldame who picked a lift up the mountain on the municipal rubbish-collector's cart. But that too changed: the beldame died, her cart was replaced by a high-powered lorry that ground up the refuse with scientific know-how. There was no more fish. Suddenly it was assumed that everyone now had a car (for this is called progress), and could do their marketing among the concrete canyons of Monte Carlo, which lies four miles west, and where steel and cement is also seen as progress. But since all the young of the village had left to live in modern blocks of small rooms called *studios de standing* – roughly 'classy pads' – the remaining inhabitants made do with the resources of THE SHOP, or, if too old, or too conservative to drive a car, had to content themselves with rattling up and down in a rickety bus which twice a day linked us to the mainstream of life along the coast – the Côte d'Azur of tourist brochures.

I am among this 'retro' band who still live much as the village elders did centuries past; but I go further, for I seldom brave the bus, and cook and eat only what I can find locally in THE SHOP, or, hard pressed, borrow from indulgent friends, or what the villagers can provide from their *terres* – literally, lands, or earth. Such *terres* are small plots spread like handkerchiefs over the steep hillside beyond the village, and owned from time immemorial by successive generations of the same families. This is family wealth in terms of vegetables, lemon and olive trees, and perhaps a few hens scratching about in the dry earth, or a goat munching among the aromatic grasses. The *terres* take the place of cottage gardens, for this close-packed mountain village, with its steep, narrow, and often stone-vaulted alley-ways has little room for gardens. At most there may be a small stone terrace or balcony overhanging the roofs below. This gives an air of austerity unknown to the more spread-out lowland villages, where green gardens merge with the open country-side.

You may wonder why I continue here in this primitive fashion – I, who do not even own a *terre*, and who am not of the village by birth, and who, to that patriarchal community, must always remain the stranger within their gates although of forty years standing among them. Let me admit that I do not live there all the year round, but the isolation and the great blue sweep of the Mediterranean lying beyond my windows always call me back in summer. Then, too, I have a certain sentimental loyalty to my midget-sized, ill-equipped kitchen which opens onto that azure sweep, for it was there I first tried my prentice hand at cooking. In 1947 my husband Romain Gary and I had acquired a ruined doll's-house-sized dwelling, perhaps once part of the Saracen fortifications, for this village was a tenth-century stronghold. When we had, at great pains, installed water, then quite a novelty unless seeping through the old roofs in a storm, and put in electricity, which trembled on and off fitfully, I set about the cookery books of Edouard de Pomiane – greatest of all practical guides. By birth Edouard Pozerski, of Polish origin, this genius of the kitchen was also an expert in the chemical and biological aspects of eating – a forerunner of today's cult of what might be called scientific gastronomy. Pomiane named the scientific principles of cookery upon which he lectured at the Pasteur Institute, 'gastrotechnology', and it was the cunningly concealed mainspring of all he wrote – concealed because all he wrote seemed as enter-taining to read as to follow practically. Thank you my venerated, adored Dr Pomiane.

I cooked at that time by Butagaz, a sort of cylinder attached to the stove which was perfectly efficient till it ran short of gas in the middle of a roast. There was no heating in the house then, for we were naïve enough to believe the Côte d'Azur was a sun-trap all winter long. Desperately, I huddled among the steaming saucepans; indefatigably, I cooked more and more hot dishes, plunging from one chaotic experiment to the next. I never left the kitchen: no other room had a bearable temperature. I learned a lot about cooking that winter. And now that I have a refrigerator, and hot water and an electric mixer too, I consider myself fully equipped. But I still use the old stove. So, reader, if you are interested to know some of the local foods I make in such restricted circumstances, suiting my menus to the local, strictly village resources, then read on.

Imagine that I am deciding on a three-course dinner for unexpected and probably unwelcome guests (for I am anti-social when I have gone to earth in the village and am wishing to write uninterrupted). What can I provide, without taking the bus down to the markets of Menton or Monte Carlo? I should probably start them off, mellow them, I'd hope, with an excellent aperitif, a local speciality made from bitter oranges: bitter, I repeat. Then, if I happened to have fresh fish, tunny or sardines around, I could make a big platter of sliced tunny fish, with rice, bananas and tomatoes, or stuff the sardines with a rice and herb filling. But as I said, fish is not often to be had. Dried, salted cod, however, I often keep in reserve; with that I might make a *brandade*. But if there were no fish I might persuade my guests to toy with hot toast spread thick with *tapénade*, a rich, swarthy, olive, anchovy, caper and garlic mixture, accompanied by radishes or spring onions and hard boiled eggs. Or I would let them try *aïgou bolido* ('boiled water', literally), a delicious garlic broth if you go for garlic. Otherwise, I might startle them with spaghetti made dynamic and unorthodox by that fiery *rouille*, a sauce usually reserved for *bouillabaisse*. In this case, I would probably sprinkle chopped nuts over the spaghetti to give it a grainy texture, and I would be very generous with the butter. This *rouille* would induce an unquenchable thirst, and the local wines would do the rest, so that my guests would now be in a benign mood, ready to enjoy the main dish and overlook the fact that there was, probably, no fish, meat, or fowl at my table.

The main dish would be either a *ratatouille*, or stuffed aubergine, or artichokes *à la barigoule*, a charmingly decorative way of presenting this vegetable, one which removes what is to me the utter boredom of tearing off those tough outer leaves and dunking them in a vinaigrette. Here the leaves are cut down to half, the whole vegetable is slightly opened to resemble a stiff green rose and the centre filled with a mixture of mushrooms, onions, and carrots. If I had time, I might make *Babajuin*, or Juinbaba, which is made traditionally for the Feast of St John on 5 June. However, the *Babajuin* involves pastry making, which I dread. Are the guests worth the struggle?

We are a notably pious village, and every traditional festival has some deep religious significance. In August, we celebrate the occasion on which the Virgin answered our prayers in the year fourteen something and saved us, or our ancestors, from the plague. Ever since, through all the centuries, there has been a special procession and feasting, and at night a ball under the speckled plane trees of the Place des Deux Frères. This rounds off everything in a robustly secular fashion – accordion music, too much *vin ordinaire*, and a lot of loving. At Easter, on Good Friday night, a macabre procession of dark, hooded figures carries a life-sized baroque statue of the dead Christ up and down the narrow alley-ways, to the beat of muffled drums and tolling bells. Then the villagers decorate the façade of each house with curious arrangements of snail shells filled with oil, which are lit and shine like hundreds of tiny candles. A prize goes to the best design or ornamentation. Niches containing little statues of the Virgin or a saint, frequently found in the old walls hereabouts, are also decorated with snail shells. Then there is the Fête de Gênet, celebrating the yellow broom, and every house and window displays bunches of this plant which blooms all over the hills, and whose strong tangle of roots once, in the Middle Ages, saved the threatened village from a great landslide. And so it goes: remembrance and history all around, and many such events commemorated by the dishes we eat, such as *Babajuin*.

Domestic dramas are also woven into the texture of our village life, and one, long-remembered, was in the best tradition of a Pagnol film. It is an incident the older villagers still recall with enjoyment. I was not there at the time, but it was told to me later with gusto. Two or three bakers ago, it seems that the baker of that moment had returned home from his all-night baking earlier than usual and caught his pretty wife *in flagrante delicto* with the local watchman. The lover fled, and the baker dragged his wife, stark naked, through the still sleeping village to the bakery, where he hauled her up onto the roof. There she crouched, naked and whimpering. Presently the villagers awoke, and it was remarkable – quite remarkable – how great was the demand for bread that morning ... *baguettes, brioches, flûtes, pain de seigle* ... the inhabitants flocked to buy and gape. Only much later was the baker persuaded to give his erring wife a blanket, and later still to lead her home. The blinds were drawn on their reconciliation, but it must have been very thorough, for the baker did not get the ovens going again for twenty-four hours, and there was not a crumb of fresh bread to be had in the whole village.

There are not a lot of sweet dishes here: the grapes, figs, and melons or oranges grown locally are enough. In winter, there is *fougasse*, eaten for the Feast of St Michael, a plump ring of *brioche* flavoured with vanilla, a dash of Kirsch, and decorated with crystallised fruits. Or, a thick creamy custard called *tian*, after the big, round earthenware dish in which it is cooked. As there are quantities of lemon trees round about, I make a variation of the classic French dessert, *pain perdu*, where slices of bread are dipped in milk flavoured with vanilla, then drained, dipped in egg, and fried in butter, with sugar to taste – by which time, any similarity to a slice of bread has vanished. I call my concoction 'Lost Lemon', by analogy with lost bread, and replace the vanilla with lemon curd, that luscious lemon cheese, the consistency of thick honey, which I make from time to time instead of jam, although lemon curd can now be found readymade on most grocers' shelves.

Then there is one truly poetic local dessert which always enthralls my guests. This is marrow-flower fritters. The yellow flowers must be picked early in the morning, before they open. They are dipped in batter, lightly fried and sugared. More classically in the Midi, these *fleurs de courgettes* are served, not as a dessert but stuffed with rice, onions and mushrooms. But I prefer to reserve them for the sweet course, for being butterfly delicate in form and flavour they go better with sugar, perhaps mixed with cinnamon, and a flick of lemon over all.

Or I might make *palaçinki* (pancakes) just because I love the Bulgarian name for them. They can be stuffed with white cream cheese; with sliced strawberries; with melon jam. ... *palaçinki* can be varied to infinity. They bring back to me my blissful Bulgarian years.

One last word: if you look, here, for any of the classic dishes of the Midi – *bouillabaisse* or *loup au fenouil* and such – you will be thwarted. Those are dishes known all over the south, from Marseille to Avignon and further inland too. But my part of the world is other, lying just behind the tourist-trampled coast between Nice and the Italian border, and is specifically *not* Provence, but Liguria a region part Italian, part French, part Saracen even in origin, with its own tradition, language, and cuisine, such as I have sketched for you.

CHAPTER 6

Bread and Velvet
Turkish Delights

The Turkish cuisine is said to be one of the world's finest, along with the Chinese and French, but it is its amalgam of other ages and far horizons, central Asian, or Arabic, reflecting the ways of both nomadic and sedentary races, that gives it so special a quality. It is a flavour the Turks imposed on conquered lands – and flavours acquired from the lands they conquered. Indeed, the *haute cuisine* of France can be challenged, in Turkey, by recipes still in use, which date from the court cuisine of the Baghdad caliphs and other remote splendours.

Around the Turkish table I see shades of Byzantine emperors and Ottoman sultans gathered beside shepherds, Seljuk warriors or Mongol tribesmen. A sumptuous dish such as *tavük gögsü* (breast of chicken pounded smooth with cream and cinnamon), the acme of sophistication, may derive from the kitchens of an Osmanli padishah at Top Kapu Serai, while another dish, equally delicious in more rustic terms, may have originated at the primitive hearth of a caravanserai deep in the wilds of Anatolia. Likewise the prevalence of yoghourt in so many Turkish recipes is held to stem from Genghis Khan's horsemen who swept down on Turkey in the eleventh century. By way of rations, they slung sacks of goat's milk from their saddles, but the violent jolting churned the milk into a substance resembling the clotted sheep or buffalo milk, *yogurtlu*, still a staple part of the nation's diet. Thus it might be said that Turkish history is written across each plate.

Turkish dishes have evocative names, sounding as deliciously as they taste . . . Bread and Velvet – the Padishah's Pleasure – Turquoise Soup – Sweetheart's Lips – along with the celebrated *imam baildi*, 'the imam who swooned' – (no doubt because the egg-plant was cooked till almost *too* delicious, causing unwise indulgence). *Moussaka*, another egg-plant and meat casserole, is found with variations all over the Middle East, in countries much influenced by Turkish cuisine. Aubergine or egg-plant (*patlajan* to Turks) is the back-bone of many differently prepared dishes. One called *karniyarik* (or split-belly) sounds less inviting than most, but Turkey has many anatomic references in the kitchen – 'ladies' navels', little round cakelets, 'ladies' thighs', *kadin budu köftesi*, very smooth, plump rissoles, being two examples of this seductive imagery. *Ekmek kâdife*, or Bread and Velvet, is another supremely voluptuous concoction, where contrasting textures are the secret of the seemingly simple dish. In Turkey, velvet was once synonymous with all that was most beautiful, most desirable and treasured: thus the old-fashioned term of endearment, 'My satin! My velvet!' The dish of that name is merely a number of small chunks of coarse textured bread, served with a large bowl of the thickest, richest clotted cream, the kind called *kaïmak*, made from buffalo milk. That's all. There are no concessions to sugar, or even rose-petal jam as we find in so many Turkish puddings. Food such as this belongs to a patriarchal and pastoral past, where a fundamental sureness of taste discovered that the grainy texture of the bread beside the suave cream would add up to uncomplicated perfection. Likewise, we may suppose, faraway Swiss peasants were similarly discovering the delights of their melted cheese and bread *fondues*.

I first encountered *ekmek kâdife* at a wedding feast held in the garden of a small restaurant at Bouna Batchi, on a hillside of the Bythinian Mount Olympus above Brusa. It had been one of Pierre Loti's favourite retreats, and indeed was far more retreated than the famous one at Eyoub, generally associated with him. As I was then re-reading *Aziyadé*, a famous book by this curious Turcophile character, I was following his shadow from place to place. Under a dense green bower, the wedding feast was in solemn progress. The Turks are quiet in joy or grief, and always hospitable. I was pressed to take a place at the long table, and supplied with a brightly painted tin plate, and wooden spoon – just the sort of things I collect to use at home. *Kücük!* (little) – *kücük tchok az* (very little) I begged as they piled my plate with bread and cream, and cream again. ... To stem the tide of Turkish hospitality I have found this phrase, among the few I possess, one of the most useful. Later, a majestic village dignitary offered to share his *tchibouk* or water-pipe with me, and to its sociable glou-glou sound we puffed away, conversing through the medium of his grandson, a rather flash boy just returned from a course of business management in Minnesota. Over there, he said, they ate Jumbo Sundaes – such sundaes ... but words failed him, and he made a sweeping gesture which, while indicating mythical dimensions for the sundaes, also contrived to dismiss *ekmek kâdife* as old-fashioned, local stuff: which is precisely why it is so desirable.

Before I launch into further descriptive flights, my pen frisking along as it recalls the various Turkish dishes I have eaten with relish – with abandon, indeed – let us consider some of the many facets which Turkey the country (food apart) has always presented to the viewer. Each one sees it according to his own eye. ... To those who once travelled there on the fabled Orient Express, it was the end of the line, the end of four days and nights speeding across Europe to reach Constantinople. To some, a halcyon voyage, to others, a claustrophobic bore. To many present-day dragooned, packaged tourists, I fancy it represents little more than the old tag, 'harems and hammams', or a place where Turkish Delight, 'the real thing', can be bought in pretty boxes, all ready to take home.

To nineteenth-century statesmen, Turkey was principal pawn across the chequer-board of Levantine, or Near Eastern politics. 'He who holds Constantinople holds the key to the East', said Napoleon, speaking for generations of warriors and conquerors who had lusted for this strategic prize.

More romantically, the early nineteenth-century dwellers in northern climes saw it as the sweet-meat oriental world of which poets and musicians sang. A greying haze of industrialisation was already spreading fast across Europe, but Constantinople still glowed – lodestar of all romanticism.

There, it seemed *bulbuls* (or nightingales) were forever warbling in cypress groves beside the Sweet Waters of Asia, where at sunset gilded *caïques* conveyed veiled charmers to imprudent assignations. ... In the Sultan's seraglio his favourites sipped sherbert, and languished, guarded by gigantic Nubian slaves, while eunuchs, dwarfs and deaf-mutes scuttled about dealing death by bow-string or scimitar. Scheherazade, and Leila and Majnoun too (though respectively hailing from Cairo and Isfahan), were all part of a jumbled oriental vision which centred round Constantinople, and star-crossed lovers, like dark deeds, added to its fascination.

> 'Tis the clime of the East; 'tis the land of the sun
> Can he smile on such deeds as his children have done?

Thus Byron, fostering the legend which sometimes was not far from the truth. It was in any case the image fixed in Western imaginations. Any talk of Turkey's cultural heritage, its noble mosques, its music, or mystic poets, like its administrative systems across the vast territories its sultans once ruled, from North Africa to the gates of Vienna, was of less account to the public. Turkey had to remain an exotic back-cloth to the luxurious indolence of Constantinople.

This was a far cry from the thrusting, thriving city which took shape when Ataturk re-named it Istanbul and wrenched it out of its picturesque torpor to meet the twentieth century's challenge.

Yet something of its former legendary aura is retained here. All the ancient glories of earlier civilisations that merge at this cross-roads are now challenged by the superb bridge which links European and Asiatic shores in a single astonishing span. It soars above the Bosphorus where the mammoth liners and oil tankers ply and where once upon a time, some say, Leander swam to join his love. Legends again, threading through the texture of daily life. Which brings me back to my subject – traditional Turkish food.

My introduction to it came at a moment calculated to make me particularly appreciative, for I first reached Istanbul immediately after four years of life in London during World War II – years of bombing and severe rationing. (We cooked with powdered egg and margarine. Oranges and bananas, like other exotic imports, vanished. Sugar, like pastries and cakes, became a cherished memory. ...) Thus when I first set foot on Turkish soil, that immediate overwhelming confrontation with plenty came as a shock. Suddenly, I felt myself transported to realms of unchecked appetites. I plunged into every excess. In a sort of shimmering aura of desire I saw the pastry-cooks' windows piled with syrupy confections. Street booths were stacked with an infinity of sticky indulgences, tawny, golden and glistening, slices of sugar-soaked breads, cream horns, tartlets filled with rose-petal jam. ... Then there were the tropical fruits. ... Oranges, lemons or figs appeared some glittering mirage. The fish market, Balik Bazaar, was a series of exquisite *natures mortes*, huge fish lying in silvery splendour on scarlet trays, with a rose, or a string of blue amulet beads arranged in each gaping maw. Meat stalls were less alluring: whole carcasses beside gruesome sheeps' heads, or indescribable innards. Such displays reminded me of the Eastern sage who said he would not make his body a sepulchre for the animal kingdom.

In those first delirious expeditions about Istanbul, I became gradually intrigued, not only by its beauty, its pearly skies and noble skyline where mosques and minarets crown each hill, but also by the strangely haunting quality of those ancient streets which lie far from the uproar of modern Pera. Such steep cobbled byways were overhung by rickety, bleached wooden houses, always close shut and sinister, where one sensed behind each latticed window a silent watcher. Then all the stories of dark doings, of erring wives sewn up in sacks and cast into the Bosphorus, of international spy rings and opium dens closed round, and nebulous terrors could only be dispelled by further indulgences at the nearest confectioners.

Walking about this city, munching noisily as I went, I would surreptitiously brush off the crumbs of, say *dilber dudağı* ('ladies' lips') as I entered the *tekké* of the whirling dervishes at Galata or, wiping treacly fingers, removed my shoes to enter the Blue Mosque. Sacred and profane. ... Between such marvels as the Byzantine mosaics of *Kahryé djami* or the Sultan's palace at Top Kapi (then closed to the public but miraculously open to me thanks to Embassy good-will) I passed long days, gazing and guzzling. In the fabled Seraglio, astonishingly alone but for an ancient custodian who soon tired of my energy and went back to doze in the gate-house, I spent many unforgettable hours of exploration and conjecture. It was not then restored, to become the superbly organised museum we know today. Alone, then, wandering at will about dark, dusty warrens, I would push open a creaking door, or climb a rotted stairway to reach shadowy realms of splendour; how could I know, then, that I stood in Sultan Murad's Throne Room, or the Corridor Where the Djinns Hold Consultation? Later, almost satiated with historic echoes, I would settle myself under a cypress tree, by the Gate of Felicity, and open a paper bag full of syrupy cakes, perhaps most suitably, *sarai lokmasi*, or Palace Fritters – felicity indeed.

And when, pray, had you eaten your fill, the diet-conscious reader may ask? The day I was on one of those steamers that zig-zag up and down the Bosphorus, from shore to shore, with energetic boys rushing about dispensing glasses of very sweet tea or small cups of Turkish coffee. On that day, and there are many such grey days in Istanbul, gales raged down from the Black Sea (which takes its name from its ill-temper, rather than its inky colour) and the Bosphorus lashed and swirled in an ugly mood. On such days the small boats lie in-shore, but the steamers plough on, reeling. Then, only then, did I discover moderation.

Today I have come to prefer the salty variety of Turkish pastry; notably such melting specialities as *börek*, a small pie-let or turnover with gauze-fine layers of flaky pastry resembling *mille-feuilles*. *Börek* are usually stuffed with white cheese and herbs, or spinach, and are served sizzling hot, before the meal proper begins. Another kind, *Tartar börek* are softer, more doughy, and boiled, for they originated in the nomad encampments of Asia Minor where cauldrons rather than ovens were usual.

Vegetables are the back-bone of the everyday Turkish meal which, sugary delights apart, is remarkably healthy and frugal. Meat is grilled, or used sparingly, as part of a vegetable ragout.

Tomatoes, *domates*, appear with monotonous regularity, stuffed, as stuffing, as sauce, as themselves, or as a salad, with raw onion rings and black olives, dressed with oil and lemon juice. Never, never with mayonnaise. Rice is treated more sparingly here than in some other countries, for it only grows in one, eastern area of Turkey, and thus remains, for the most part, an imported delicacy used for stuffing vegetables, for pilaffs, or the classic stuffed vine leaves. All this about vegetables, but what about ways with eggs and fish? Well, eggs are eggs everywhere, boiled, fried or as omelettes: though one Turkish way of serving them poached, and covered with yoghourt is not for me. Fish is usually grilled or threaded on skewers, *shish kebab* fashion. (*Shish* means sword or spit.)

With *döner kebab*, we return to meat, and with it the true splendour of Turkish cooking. Not that it is a complicated dish, in itself, being plain roast lamb, but it is the fashion in which it is achieved which renders it so delectable. Restaurants, whether lordly or lowly, like the smallest *lokantas* that are tucked away, or even those recess-like street booths, just an oven in the wall, become known for the excellence of their *döner kebab*. Devotees come from afar to relish its succulence, sometimes standing in the street, to eat it 'on the hoof', or taking slices away, wrapped in pitta bread.

Döner kebab is found all across the Middle East, but it is essentially

Turkish, its preparation always following complicated traditional methods. First, the boned meat is marinated for twenty-four hours in yoghourt, with oil, vinegar, onions, tomatoes and herbs added. Next, sliced thinly and loaded, slice by slice, onto a tall, perhaps three-foot high vertical spit. (Sometimes, the slices are alternated with finely minced meat mixed with fat from one of those majestic fat-tailed sheep that are so esteemed in this part of the world.) When all is tightly packed onto the spit, and resembles a bulging sausage, it is placed in front of the three-tiered oven, which is composed of metal trays one on top of the other, each tray containing glowing charcoal. As the spit revolves and the outside layers of lamb are cooked, they are shaved off in wafer-thin slices, leaving an inner layer to take its turn before the fire. And so it goes, until the last diminished morsel is sliced off, and the whole process of preparation must begin again.

Tavuk gögsü is one of the most ceremonial of all Turkish dishes, but rarely made correctly today, I am told, like the real *boeuf stroganov*, once the peak of Russian cooking. *Tavuk gögsü* is breast of chicken beaten to a smooth pulp, which is then poached in milk, with sugar added and also some mysterious herb (not revealed to me), till it becomes a firm, but yielding mass. Powdered with cinnamon, and served with cream it ranks among the more legendary Turkish puddings. I have never eaten it myself, but I am told the presence of meat, or rather chicken, is perfectly undetectable.

Finally, to round off my appreciation of the Turkish table I must add that its *presentation* is part of the pleasure it offers. As everywhere in the Orient, the eye is always tempted as much as the belly. There is an old story which tells of a sultan who learned that one of his viziers lived in even greater style than he did, which was not to be countenanced. The sultan made a surprise visit to the vizier, and was entertained royally at a long and exquisite banquet. At the end, elaborately carved bowls containing a refreshing fruit compote were handed round. But to the sultan's astonishment, the bowls began melting away, their intricate ornamentation vanishing, curlicue by crystal curlicue. When the sultan learned that the vizier's cook was in the habit of carving such bowls himself, fashioning them from blocks of ice, each day a fresh design suited to the fruit in question, he was obliged to admit his own kitchens could not compete with such luxurious refinements.

And it is just this awareness of beauty, this *will* to expend great care and thought on the decorative aspects of each dish, however simple, that plays so important a part in the traditions of the Turkish table.

CHAPTER 7

Count Rumford's Soup and Some Others

O ur daily soup being, to my mind, almost as important as our daily bread, who better to head this piece than the philanthropic and ingenious Count who fed a couple of thousand beggars and starving outcasts at the cost of a ha'penny a head? Moreover, he fed them well, for the principles of nutrition, calorie content and such were one of his numerous interests. But there was more to the count than that. Much more. This remarkable character, born Benjamin Thompson in Massachusetts in 1753, early became celebrated as a *Wunderkind* of scientific bent. At fourteen his command of algebra, astronomy and higher mathematics astounded the savants. During the War of Independence, when the British army withdrew from Boston, his sympathy with England decided him to emigrate. Established in London, his scientific achievements won him a knighthood from George III. Later, a chance meeting with the Elector of Bavaria, Prince Maximilian, led him to become that ruler's Grand Chamberlain, Minister of War and of the Police. The Elector recognised ability when he saw it. Soon, he conferred the Holy Roman Empire title of count on Sir Benjamin, who chose the name Rumford from an American township he remembered with affection.

The count's various achievements at the Elector's court were crowned by his improvements in the living conditions of the poor, and the reduction of the enormous number of beggars and thieving vagrants who plagued the land. This he did by first housing and feeding them (which is where his soup came in) and then setting them to useful and remunerative trades. How sound his philanthropic philosophy: 'To make a vicious and unhappy people content, it is first thought necessary to make them virtuous. But why not first make them content? Then virtue may well follow.' In Bavaria, during his life there, he saw these beliefs put into action

successfully, for his soup was not only nutritious but palatable too –
something of which public institutions such as hospitals and schools
might well take notice, their brews being usually dingy slops resembling washing-up water.

The count's miraculous soup is much the same as one concocted
two centuries earlier, by St Vincent de Paul when he was a parish
priest in Paris, where he also created the first Foundling hospital at
Clichy, and with his Sisters of Charity struggled against the appalling
poverty then prevailing.

From the earliest times, soup, in one form or another, has always
been the staple, and sometimes sole sustenance for the various tribes
of Central Asia. Gonzales de Clavijo's meticulous account of his
diplomatic mission to the court of Tamerlane describes the gargantuan feasts served in those sable-lined, scarlet tents of the great
khan. There are also accounts of how the warriors of the different
hordes, the Blue, the White, or the Golden, could sustain life in
hard times on a bleak-sounding brew. When times were easy, says
Clavijo, the hordes gorged on night-long feasts of roasted meat,
mutton, or horse-flesh, with sugared breads. But in lean times they
lived, or rode to battle, on a mixture of sour milk tempered with
water. Small cakes of flour and water were kneaded and baked, and
hung from the warriors' saddles. When the hordes camped, these
cakes were thrown into a vinegary broth, which, in the treeless
steppes, was heated over fires of compressed cattle dung.

As I am addicted to all manner of soups, finding them the most
comforting and practical of foods, I have fallen into the habit of
making some kind of fresh vegetable soup every two or three days.
And then, it gives me an opportunity to use some of the charming
old tureens I have collected, elegant white and gold Empire, Mason's
Ironstone, or painted tin urns from Afghanistan street markets.
Soup ladled at table, from a tureen, and into a little china bowl, at
once assumes style – a homely majesty denied it when awash in a
soup plate. And I ignore any etiquette which pronounces soup at
luncheon as inadmissible – vulgar.

Alexis Soyer, the great chef whose legend still illuminates the
Reform Club kitchens, which he designed, always added a little
sugar and vinegar to vegetable soups, to bring out the flavour.
Soyer, like Count Rumford, was both philanthropic and inventive.

During the appalling Crimean War of 1853–6, he rushed out to Scutari to join Florence Nightingale in her titan's struggle to ameliorate the wretched soldiers' lot. Between them, and aided by Soyer's specially designed stove 'The Gastronomic Regulator', orderly kitchens (like organised wards) gradually emerged from the chaos and filth that was killing off the wounded faster than grapeshot. And soups – nourishing broths, on the lines of Count Rumford's, were the great stand-by.

As competition to those sumptuous soups such as vichyssoise, turtle or lobster bisque (mostly tinned today), let us consider a truly royal dish, once known as Queen Victoria's Soup. Few of us will attempt it, exquisite as it sounds, for it demands three plump fowls, a strong veal broth, the yolks of six hard-boiled eggs, ground almonds, a quart of cream, French rolls, and even the humble parsley. In the first heady days of the Queen's reign, Her Majesty's chef was Francatelli, an Italian born in England, but trained by the illustrious Carême, and Queen's Soup is attributed to him.

The young Queen Victoria revelled in the luxuries of court life, tasted for the first time after her astringent upbringing. Gone the sago puddings and lamb chops of Kensington Palace; gone the restrictive presence of her mother. She savoured her chef's finest flights along with the fascinating conversation of her premier, Lord Melbourne. He was always seated beside her, protocol or no; that was her decree. She hung on his words; he was so wise, so entertaining, so *experienced*. ... Yet Lord Melbourne's sybaritic tastes often led him to imprudent indulgences at table. However, as long as he was beside the Queen, although she chided him, she would linger while he demolished yet another ice or dozed over his wine.

Later, many years later, the Queen grew indifferent to fine dishes and time-consuming meals. Even her most devoted courtiers admitted she bolted her food, leaving the table before her entourage had enjoyed more than a few mouthfuls of each successive course. Famished and resentful they took to midnight snacks, concealed in their bedrooms. No memoirs I have ever read disclose the nature of these snacks. Were they snatched from the table surreptitiously, and stowed in some kind of doggy bag derived from a beaded reticule, or were they obtained later, from a sympathetic flunkey? The Queen became increasingly impatient with *dîners de circonstance*, and the inexorable succession of courses. Her rather bulging, but hooded eyes observed the diners without sympathy. She was yearning for some faraway Scottish picnic, or the whisky and haggis made holy by happier times at Balmoral, with Albert.

Some of the nicest soups derive from left-overs. I do not mean the chicken-carcass type of classic; rather the sort of scraps that are usually too soon consigned to the dustbin. I am remembering the sort of mystery soups my lamented Dutch friend, Herman Schrijver, used to devise for his delighted guests. He was both gourmet and inspired cook; moreover, although well-heeled, he was thrifty and abhorred waste. But he knew just how far to go, mixing, say, some sad string beans,half a cooked kidney, a cold potato and some wilted cucumber, which with a mysterious jellied sauce and all else went into the mixer with lemon – always some lemon in Herman's concoctions. It emerged, delicious and defying analysis ... sherry, cream, or a little curry might be added at whim. I have followed his methods in loving, greedy memory.

As I seldom eat meat, or have bones around, I must confess to relying on those despised cubes of chicken or vegetable bouillon when in need of something approaching a meat stock. Stealthily blended with herbs, onions, or whatever, they pass muster, and indeed, are blessed, in this household. Tinned soups in general I consider odious, with the exception of one brand of *consommé en gelée*. Frozen soups are a better buy, if you must ... but must you?

Although I make almost every kind of vegetable soup, I have always baulked at avocado, recalling a journey across Yucatan where they prevailed at every meal. Reaching Progresso (then a dump town, rather inaptly named) Romain and I tried to escape the blistering heat by bathing in a stretch of warm, opaque, curiously mustard-coloured sea. We had lunched on avocados, we knew they would be there for dinner; but we had not reckoned on large heaps of them, over-ripe and rotting along the beach, where enormous long-legged crabs scuttled.

Years passed, and suddenly, avocados appeared on the European market and I was offered them, inevitably, inescapably, with or without shrimps, with a vinaigrette, with tomatoes, anchovies, hard boiled eggs, curried sauce, or even mayonnaise. But I remained firmly anti-avocado, until a friend converted me by her avocado soup, a soft green, delicate, yet not insipid masterpiece (see p. 141). It conjures for me another, kinder tropical scene, the sort of palm-fringed shores, as rendered by eighteenth-century scenic wallpapers where, in bowers of passion-flowers and frangipani, brightly plumed birds flitter, and turtles sport amorously, unthreatened by Aldermen's banquets or a Heinz tin.

A last word on soups in general. They must be very hot or *very* cold. Tepid is inadmissible. The friend of a friend of a friend of mine stood no half measures in his Castle Rack-Rent Irish dwelling. 'Soup's cold!' he would announce to the assembled table, and proceed to hurl the tureen out of the window, the company following suit with their soup plates. Whole sequences of priceless china went that way, strewing the grassy slopes to the lake, into which fragments were presently cast. They formed a mosaic in the mud, over which the fish swam indifferently.

CHAPTER 8

Russian Traditional

W e are apt to think of Russian food as the caviar of princes, or the black bread of bitterness such as Gorky's characters ate with cabbage soup and little else. But there was, and still remains in some parts of the Soviet Union, a traditional, provincial cuisine. It varies as much as the climate or countryside and it is such variations I always tried to discover on my journeys about the USSR. ... Down the Volga to Astrakhan, or to the Siberian–Mongolian border, by way of the legendary Trans-Siberian train, to the *aôuls*, mountain villages of the Caucasus, or the *tchai-khanas* or tea-houses of Samarkand and Khiva, such local dishes were still to be found. Some of my findings I will describe here. But first let me say that I do not imply one could never eat well in Moscow or Leningrad. As a visitor I did – but the big hotels were slanted to the tourist hordes, with an internationalised mass cuisine more often than those localised dishes which I love immoderately. To me, typical traditional Russian cooking is perhaps the best of all: you may keep your Chinese rice or French soufflés: give me some of those age-old and rustic delights of the Russian provinces which recall the spreads so lovingly described by nineteenth-century Russian authors, the kind expatriates still contrive.

I have sometimes wondered if my especial fondness for Russian food and the abiding presence of a samovar in my home is not due to my childhood reading, which was largely concentrated on such authors as Leskov, Gogol, Saltikov-Schredin and those who dwelt on life in the provinces. Even today, when I re-read *Dead Souls*, and follow Chichigov as his *britchka* rattles from one forgotten country town to another, I am impatient for him to reach his next stop, where Gogol will make my mouth water with descriptions of the feast – sucking pig with horse-radish and cream, or *oukha*, a special kind of fish soup, *blinnii*, or cray fish, and a mushroom *pirog*, or pie.

The lesser giants of Russian literature, such as Aksakov, often dwell on the pleasures of a pastoral repast eaten in a little wooden *izba* dwelling. I wonder, should I enjoy Melnikov-Pechersky's pawky descriptions of the Old Believers so much, were it not for his minute accounts of those gargantuan feasts which they still contrived during the Lenten fasts? Over every page hangs the pungent odour of salted fish and dill pickles. But as the nineteenth century proceeded, and more widely known Russian authors emerged, there was a marked decline in descriptive gastronomic flights. . . . It was the soul, rather than the belly, which now inspired them. Turgenev's wan gentry sat round samovars, as every Russian has always done, but their menus are generally left to our imagination. Chekhov's characters sighed out their sorrows or ennuis rather than fed them in the robust manner of the repulsive Golovliev family. And in the twentieth century both stomachs and souls gave place to political idealism and the black bread of bitterness that Gorky and later writers have used as a symbol of oppression.

I once had the good fortune to have a Russian cook: we were living in California at the time, but in no time at all, our kitchen had that authentic, all-pervading smell of salted fish, poppy seed, and some indefinable leathery, fishy aroma which is all Russia. Katyusha made classic delights such as *koulibiac*, a long pastry turnover filled with salmon, rice, and cabbage; or *paskha*, an Easter speciality, a cone of cream, cheese, raisins and almonds. She used to torment me with descriptions of a dish of ham, *boujenina* which had to be cooked with wine, and a truss of hay. We never achieved this, as it seemed difficult to find anything so rural as hay in motorised Hollywood. Perhaps I should have gone to the studios specialising in Westerns. Why didn't I think of that?

Among the Russian dishes I have most enjoyed when travelling in the USSR would be *omoul*, a subtle-flavoured firm-fleshed white fish found in the fathomless waters of Lake Baikal, 'the Holy Sea'. Like sturgeon or *osetrina*, *omoul* is so good that it requires no fancy treatment and is usually poached, and eaten with plenty of butter. But since it is a purely local delicacy, I will describe some Russian ways of stuffing more available fish, thus making even the insipid cod more interesting. Try it stuffed with sultanas, celery, onions and parsley, all bound with sour cream, the whole stewed in cider.

Or fresh tunny fish slices covered in a thick sauce of sharp cheese, nutmeg and sour cream again, baked in a little oil and vinegar.

In Siberia, apart from fishy delights, there was a fiery range of meat dishes, such as *boeuf stroganov* which was made famous abroad by the celebrated gourmet Count Stroganov, but which takes its name originally from the word *strogat* – to shred. It is composed of shredded beef, and a mustardy sauce of strength, thus an invitation to unscrupulous cooks to disguise poor meat – not that such a thing was done when I ate it in Irkutsk at a party for a Buriat Mongol football team. They were there to play against Irkutsk United but were all agog to know more about 'the Tweest' and wished me to translate the words of a record they cherished 'Baby! Let's twist again!' I did my best, and was later invited to a Buriat wedding in the Asiatic hinterland near Kiahtka, about which I remember very little, for the drinks were fierce. I asked for *koumiss*, the miraculous, health-giving fermented mare's milk of the steppes, enjoyed by such vigorous persons as Genghis Khan and Tolstoy. Although there were some mares tethered beside the jeeps, outside the felt-covered yurts where we caroused, I was fobbed off with Armenian brandy and some local liqueur. It would have been wiser to have stuck to *kvass*, a traditional Russian beer-like brew composed of fermented black bread, sultanas and a sprig of mint. My hang-over lasted two days and left me in a state of Dostoievskian repentance.

Apropos bread – what white bread can compare with the classic Russian kind? Ah! that white bread – those plaited loaves, snow white and close-textured which eat chunkily, as kidney does. Russian delicatessens in Paris keep up the tradition, thus wooing away many bread-eating French from the baguette – corner-stone of their every meal.

In the early sixties in Moscow and Leningrad, one could obtain a thick square of this white bread with a dollop of caviar on top, as a snack between acts at the opera or ballet. It was washed down with a glass of vodka or tea; even so, such snacks were moderately priced – that is, available to citizens as well as visitors. (Or they were so before pollution started playing up the sturgeon, with each opposing Caspian shore, Russian or Iranian, insisting pollution had begun on the far side.) Those theatre snacks I have described were easy to handle, sustaining, and added a festive touch. Apropos snacks, ice-cream was also seen as such in the USSR, where it was just as good – dare I say it? – as the American kind. Nor did sub-zero temperatures affect the demand. I have seen Soviet citizens muffled to the eyes, fur capped and booted, plodding along the snowy streets while relishing an ice-cream cone. They say ices fortify their teeth against the even icier cold around them.

Of course, *where* one eats affects one's palate: thus an ugly dining-room can breed indigestion while some indifferent dishes appear perfection if eaten in romantic or historic surroundings. The scene provides the sauce. I see myself again, sitting on a rickety wooden balcony overhanging the river Kür at Tiflis; my friends have ordered a specially rustic dish for me, *kalajosh*, a stew of lamb and bread cubes fried in oil with onions and accompanied by yoghourt. I am eating this with special emotion, because they tell me that Lermontov, their tragic, demoniac and dashing poet, used to enjoy it here, before a senseless duel did for him in 1841. At home, that same dish would just have been mutton stew. Yes, ambiance is all. ... Now while meat pies are meat pies are meat pies, as Gertrude Stein might have said, had she eaten them as I did, under the dappled shade of the great plane trees beside Tamerlane's tomb in Samarkand, she might have been more expansive.

There they are called *manti*, and are small short-pastry turnovers filled with lamb or goat meat and local herbs. They are sold at street corners or in the markets of the Tadjik and Uzbeg Republics, and cooked in a curious manner by being thrown onto the red-hot sides of huge Ali-Baba jars, where they cling, until dislodged on a long two-pronged stick. Like the classic Russian *piroshki*, of which they are country cousins, they are delicious. I used to buy several, and with half a luscious, cannon-ball-sized melon, for which this region is famous, I would repair to a *tchai-khana*, or tea-house, there to sit cross-legged among the shaggy fur-capped, or flat-capped figures, a handsome Uzbeg or Tadjik assembly – all men, for women are by custom absent here. However, being a tourist, I did not count as such, or indeed as being entirely human, I fancy: there were few tourists in such regions at that time, and those who appeared were regarded rather as visitors from Outer Space.

It is held that an Uzbeg man is no man if he cannot prepare certain special dishes for grand occasions, and I longed to ask for recipes, but the language barrier rose between us and only smiling pantomime remained. ('Cook till delicious' once again.) It was a friendly scene, all of us drinking tea from little blue bowls, with a flowery teapot apiece, a custom which lends an air of timeless hospitality to cafés all across Central Asia, from the Hindu Kush to the Caspian. Would the meat pie and melon have seemed quite so exquisite, eaten elsewhere? The proximity of Tamerlane's turquoise tomb may have added zest to the feast.

What other special regional Russian dishes do I recall lovingly, but which are not necessarily inextricably interwoven with their setting? *Blini*, of course, now an international delight, soaked in melted butter, with cream added, and no thought of the silhouette, or the morrow. By tradition, one should end the *blini*-feast with a bowl of blazing hot bouillon, 'to cut the fat', as gourmands say hopefully. I suppose the basic ingredients for the abiding Russian cuisine would still be cabbage, dill pickles, sour cream (*smetana*), mushrooms, buckwheat groats (*kasha*), and salted herrings (*selodka*). The *zakouska*, or hors-d'œuvres platter, once always began the meal. *Zakouska* offers any number of inventive flights, as well as the classic pickled mushrooms, black radishes, little sausages, cheese, smoked sturgeon and caviar for the fortunate. The sort of dips of cauliflower-lets and mayonnaise, or potato crisps in an egg-plant purée which seem usual at American gatherings, pale beside a Russian dip made from mixing herring fillets with grated onion, sour cream and hard boiled eggs, plus tart green apples or gooseberries. Salted fish, anchovies especially, sometimes appear in the most unlikely manner, as in a recipe for roast chicken, of which I have heard but not encountered. It seems one mixes an anchovy butter, to stuff the chicken, and mashes some more fillets into the gravy round the bird, before serving. To be tried out with caution, I think, but no prejudice.

Many traditional dishes such as *golubtsi* ('little pigeons') are ground beef, pork, onion and rice wrapped in cabbage leaves – fiddling to make, like *pilmeny*, a suety sort of boiled *manti*, which in the Ukraine is sweet, eaten with jam, but in Siberia is smaller, filled with meat, more like ravioli. In winter it hangs outside the house in grape-like bunches, frozen stiff by the climate, to be broken off bit by bit, as required – Siberia's answer to the deep-freeze.

I have particularly enjoyed the enormous variety of vegetable dishes found in Russia. Plain boiled potatoes are my staple and also theirs; country folk eat them with a mushroom or dill sauce:

Georgians add their walnut sauce, *satsivi*, which is also added to carrots or spinach. And then, there are so many ways of cooking cucumber: poached with sour cream and dill, baked with a cheese sauce, scalloped with hard boiled eggs; or raw with yoghourt, and a lot of garlic slivers added, as a cold summer soup. Which reminds me that nothing about the Russian cuisine should ignore *stchee* – cabbage soup, a filling and all-pervading dish, which can be made two ways – one, a twenty-four hour job, with meat, like the best *bortsch*; another, far simpler and quicker, is meatless, such as one given me by Madame Vera Stravinsky when she and the composer were living near me in Hollywood (see p. 143).

The Russian tradition of *zakouska* – starters, in today's lingo – has always been widely known: less so, the charming way of meeting for a last late glass of tea, around ten or eleven o'clock, with perhaps some little cakes or fruit, or a glass of fruit cordial. *Vercherum tchai* – the evening tea, was once a national custom, and faithfully continued in the many émigré households I have known throughout my life. Gathered round the magnetic presence of the samovar, the company thrashed out political niceties, the children's progress at school, or the dramas of their hearts and souls, as they sipped tea from glasses encased in filigree silver or metal holders (try holding a glass of hot tea without). No milk or sugar went with the tea, but the most delicious spoonfuls of home-made preserves – raspberry, cherry, or the like – overcrowded the saucer, where the spoon balanced precariously. It was all part of the evening's ritual. Nor had this entirely vanished from the USSR I knew both before and after World War II. Although the tea was often without much aroma, and perhaps there was no jam, there would be little home-made cakey biscuits, which instantly imparted a festive air. When I was invited by Shostakovich to a gathering of musicians after a performance – or was it the première – of his opera, *The Lady Macbeth of Mtsensk*, *vercherum tchai* still produced some timeless atmosphere of content. No outside pressures intruded, and over all the samovar presided, national emblem and essential presence, humming and puffing softly in the Green Room of the Bolshoi – or was it the Mariinsky? – as another one was no doubt doing in some snow-bound *izba*. Or, as yet another of its kind still does, beneath a purple-flowering jacaranda tree in my southern garden.

When Sir Sydney Cockerell arrived at Yasnaya Polyana to visit

Tolstoy, he found the whole family in the garden (beside the samovar of course) enjoying cucumber sandwiches. But theirs were a Slav variation on the theme, the sandwiches being spread with honey as well as the sliced cucumbers. ... An audacious mixture: though I fancy the mixture might be better and even more audacious, were the cucumbers the *pickled* kind beloved of every Russian, and one of Tolstoy's most irresistible temptations.

CHAPTER 9

The Wilder Shores
of Picnicking

Picnics are a repast to which my title best applies. The wildest, most improbable things, eaten out of doors, preferably in some remote setting, seem absolutely right and put to shame the uninspiring cold chicken and thermos flasks which nestle so smugly in the well-equipped picnic-baskets of convention.

Picnics have always been part of the English scene. Ginger biscuits and a thermos of sloshy tea with Nanny, on some bracing beach. The midnight dormitory feasts of school-days, cocoa, sardines and sausages. Romantic picnics in punts, at Henley Regatta; elaborate hampers at Glyndbourne; tea-urns at Lords. Etonian excesses on the fourth of June. Hampers full of sustenance for those banging away in the butts on 'the glorious twelfth' (though some of us find the adjective inappropriate when applied to that organised slaughter which goes by the name of sport). And finally there is our present-day adaptation of the picnic, now domesticated, or brought indoors in terms of the TV dinner-snack, a tray full of mysterious cartons and fast foods, or unwisely ambitious versions of Irish stew or trifle, to accompany those singular versions of life to which the Box has accustomed the British, as well as the American public.

I do not believe other European countries are quite so spell-bound by the Box, as yet. The French nation as a whole, for example, has not yet abandoned that sacrosanct act of sitting round the dinner table. Télé trays have not made much headway at present. Nor does this most traditional of people accept picnics other than as an organised transfer of the dining-room to the open air. (Manet's delightful group under the trees, with the naked lady and the picnic spread was probably wishful thinking.) Thus, those curiously formal roadside repasts to which French motorists aspire, and which can be observed all along the sweeping mileage of their *routes nationales*, are faithful extensions of the homes they have just left. Pitched close to the back of their car, by means of folding tables and chairs, tablecloths, cutlery, china, glass, and even *changements des vins,* they reconstruct the dining-room they have reluctantly left. The French generally mistrust Nature, particularly eating in its midst, since meal-times are still taken seriously, in spite of a growing fashion among the young to adopt casual Americanisms, *le snack, le coke, le hot dog,* or the new fast food restaurants which are ousting the bistro, and offering speed before standards. Which is a pity, for with this nation's great gastronomic traditions and sense of what is fitting – *le style* in all things, they might have come up with some splendid picnic menus.

I wonder. Could this lack of invention be due, in part, to the Code Napoléon? By its decrees MAN still dominates, legally and domestically, in spite of a number of new, much disputed reforms. The Frenchmen I have observed, and indeed men of most other races too, dislike picnics. It is a curious male characteristic. ... Men prefer to concentrate on what they are eating, and are distracted by scenery and insects – wasps especially, which they provoke unnecessarily by flapping at them instead of calming them by a few tempting titbits on the side. Man is disorientated by not being seated at the table (at its *head,* of course). And of course, detests having to lug the hamper to some remote and romantic site selected by the females of the party.

I was brought up to believe no meal could be eaten indoors if it was possible to be eaten outside, in the garden, on a balcony or wherever the sky was all around. I remember raw, winter days of watery sunshine when my mother, a fragile woman, wrapped in rugs and wearing woolly gloves, presided over rapidly congealing luncheons on our terrace overlooking the Thames. While this might have conditioned me to loathe al fresco eating, it did not, and I still feel stifled indoors, or in those restaurants which deny daylight, with table lamps and heavy curtains. Therefore, I am a natural for picnics, something made easier by the fact that I live in one of the best climates in the world.

On my travels, which are largely directed towards torrid zones, I am able to continue al fresco eating, while noting some of the foods that can be easily echoed at home. Echoed, alas! For nothing ever can replace the joys of eating impromptu meals in some wild and lovely setting. .... Generally local foods, eaten by the wayside are more interesting than anything served in hotels or restaurants *en route*. In lands considered 'under-developed' (in today's patronising phrase) – life is still geared for the nomad or passer-by. No need to take much of a picnic basket along the Golden Road to Samarkand.

In the pine-dark forests of Bavaria, the mad King Ludwig II knew all about the pleasures of picnicking, and contrived the *ne plus ultra* in picnic menus, or so he saw them, when he took to dashing about his kingdom by night – one-night stands generally – the destination being decided on the spur of the moment. This capricious monarch would usually only eat one meal, or sleep one night, in any of his numerous palaces, hunting-lodges or grandiose architectural fantasies, before dashing on again.

But the whole thing was a cheat, picnic-wise, for a retinue of cooks, scullions, pages and grooms had to precede his torch-lit sleigh with its plumed white horses caracoling across the snow. The minions were compelled to go at an even more furious pace, in order to arrive well before the king, to set up every imaginable luxury, gold plate, crystal, china, portable ovens and lavish ingredients for spectacular spreads. Here is a typical royal menu, as cited in a curious book I possess, written by one of the royal scullions.

MENU

17 October

Sweetbread soup
Gooseliver on toast

Fried carp with parmesan sauce

Roast veal stuffed with kidney, anchovy and sour cream
Roebuck stewed in cider
Semolina dumplings

Nut cake with rum and chocolate sauce
Troubled thoughts *(a sugar-iced biscuit)

Beer and champagne

*which might well follow such a menu.

All very fine and large, but hardly a picnic. Now for some more modest suggestions.

The foods I shall suggest on p.147 do away with much fuss, for they are designed to be eaten cold: no thermos flasks or spirit lamps. I only call on a combination cork-screw-knife as essential. Which reminds me of an English picnic, long ago, in Cornwall, where of course we took along Cornish pasties. We also took a bottle of vintage claret. It was a bitter spring day, and the wine cried out to be *chambré*. I was made to stumble across the moors mulling it in my bosom. When it was judged to be at the prescribed room temperature, we sat down to the feast – only to find we had forgotten the corkscrew.

As for other essentials (unless you are convivial enough to pass the bottle round for a swig), there is the question of glasses – paper cups, or plastic mugs. I feel strongly on this point. Picnics should have an air of careless luxury. Little silver *timbales*, or the classic horn drinking-cups, often silver-mounted, which were once part of hunting field equipment, are elegant and practical. During a time when I was travelling constantly and in remote areas, a time when life seemed one long joyous picnic, I used to drink from the silver christening mugs I had collected along with those old-fashioned christening-present sets of spoon, knife and fork designed to start the toddler off in style. They were usually initialled, with mother-of-pearl or bone handles, and were also extremely practical, the small flat leather case in which they fitted being no trouble *en route*. Although some critics said such refinements were absurd on the road to Timbuctu or wherever, I always had the feeling that they – the spoons and forks and mugs – enjoyed such exotic outings after years of high-chair nursery ennui.

There are certain picnickers of an uncomplicated nature who claim cold pork chops accompanied by raw apple are the perfection of al fresco eating: and being the outdoor version of roast pork and apple sauce, they are certainly more virile than cold roast chicken. There is also the straightforward pork pie, the classic being a Melton Mowbray, which has sustained generations of hard-riding squires in the English hunting field. Apropos pork chops, and their reputation for indigestibility, I am reminded that Lord Palmerston, Queen Victoria's octogenarian statesman, downed three for breakfast the day he died; nor were they cited by his doctors as cause of death.

The funeral baked meats of Biblical association might seem a far cry from picnics, yet when I lived in Bulgaria, centuries of Turkish domination had left a curious mixture of faiths, Orthodox and Moslem, causing the mixed population each to nourish their grief in an al fresco fashion. Leaving the rich candle-lit darkness of an Orthodox church with black robed monks chanting beside an open coffin where the corpse lay, waxy and remote, I would be accosted by numbers of bunchy shawled figures, ancient beldams offering, in the name of the departed, delicious little cakelets. These were eaten ritually, while crossing oneself and offering a sort of Resurrection kiss to the mourners, and later, the corpse, at the graveside.

The Moslem burial ground was generally on an open hillside, commanding some beautiful distance, as if to console. There, as in Turkey, I often came on those traditional graveside feasts where the mourners enjoy the departed's favourite food and, between mouthfuls and prayers, implore him to return to enjoy it with them. Death, the parting of the ways, is not regarded by Islam with the lugubrious relish of some other religions. Thus, the heirloom cemetery rug is spread, and the whole family, grandfathers, mothers, uncles, cousins and babies linger there till dusk, and the last of the pious picnic has been eaten in quiet communion with the lost and loved.

But now, a last word on food for the more usual, or secular picnics we were discussing earlier. I am against most salads. Few stand up to picnic conditions. Dressed lettuce wilts; undressed, it is positively indecent. However celery, tomatoes and cucumbers are naturals. (Don't forget the salt.) In rugged countries where fearful diseases follow on eating raw vegetables, I make do with peeled tomatoes, raw onions and a pinch of sugar and lemon juice, all mixed by the roadside. Or I rescue an avocado from boredom by sprinkling it with slivers of raw onion.

Shish kebab being essentially a hot dish I don't recommend it here, for as I said, I'm for picnics where nothing has to be cooked or re-heated. But *fish kebab* works well cold. Thread the skewer with chunks of any firm cooked fish – salmon or swordfish are best – alternating with tomato, bay leaf and lemon. Brush over with a sharp oil and vinegar dressing and wrap each *kebab* skewer in its own twist of foil for the journey. This is a favourite dish in the little restaurants along the Bosphorus. We used to order them, and then eat them in our caïque, floating timelessly beside the Sweet Waters of Asia, our pleasure sharpened by a bottle of fiery raki, a Pernod-like spirit.

Ham? The most banal slices of ham can be made intriguing if wrapped cornucopia fashion round Liptauer, a firm cream cheese, which is beaten up with capers, chopped onions, or sometimes anchovies, to which much paprika is added, giving it a pinkish tinge. On a sheep farm lost in the Puzta, the great plains of Hungary, I enjoyed such cornucopias made with slices or raw, home-cured ham; these were alternated with cold green peppers, similarly stuffed, the outside being burnt or singed by being held over a flame to obtain a smoky flavour. (Of course, the fiery seeds inside must be carefully removed before stuffing.) In this case, the peppers are only half-cooked – firm, and perfect for picnics, but tough on some digestions perhaps. If cooked through, in sauce, they are too collapsed for transport and should be eaten hot, and indoors at that.

All this, and nothing for sweet-tooths tired of apple and banana hand-outs? Then what could be more sublime than American cheese-cake – unless it is the English Christmas pudding? This, eaten cold, like cake, is an all-the-year round joy. So is Turkish Delight, lurking rosily beneath its sugary bloom; or Elvas plums, glistening dark mouthfuls in their gold lace-paper frills. Each makes an elegant, festive ending to the feast. And if most of my suggestions seem tough on the waistline, remember, picnics, being occasional rather than regular, should have no concern with diets.

CHAPTER 10

The Turquoise Table
Traditional Persian Food

Persia, the Turquoise Kingdom of legend and history, is now called Iran, though we still continue to speak of Persian carpets and Persian miniatures (or the Persian Gulf, for that matter). I always think of the lovely land I knew as Persia, and ask indulgence to write of it thus.

My introduction to traditional Persian food took place many years ago, in a country house on the slopes of the Elburz mountains, deep in the woods north of Teheran. It belonged to an aged general, and all was tradition there. The rather ramshackle house, with its tall pillared and recessed verandah or *talah,* where a samovar purred ceaselessly, recalled those nests of gentlefolk which Turgenev describes. It was a patriarchal life, at once rural and intellectual. One of the finest private libraries of the Middle East was housed a few steps from the cow-sheds. The atmosphere was both careless and welcoming, with a sort of battered luxury added. There were big iron stoves to heat the rooms, ancient rugs and worn scraps of rare embroideries everywhere, and a piano stacked with the scores of Russian operas. There were horses in the stables, and cows in the pasture, for my hostess (of English origin) had been the first to introduce fresh cow's milk to Iran: earlier there was only goat's or ewe's milk (the latter makes what is unquestionably the richest, most suave yoghourt). There were also twenty or more dogs, for any stray animal always found a home there.

Once, before my time, there had been a wolf cub who grew up among the dogs, wagged his tail and did not know he was otherwise. When the family left on a long journey, they gave the gardener money and instructions to feed the wolf well. Needless to say, the gardener pocketed the money and left the wolf to fend for itself. Resourcefully, the wolf made a meal of the gardener's child. The child recovered, but the wolf was shot. On his return the general sacked the gardener – it was the least he could do to defend the wolf's memory.

Cooking in this household was strictly traditional, like the placing of the kitchen or cook-house, a building apart, in the garden. There the cook had all his equipment and cool, stone-hewed larders. Everything was prepared on big wood fires outside, under the trees, with huge iron and copper cauldrons and racks suspended over the flames. In the heavy snows of winter, a lean-to shed sheltered the fire, and the cook crunched about, muffled and swearing vigorously. But no-one ever thought of an indoor kitchen. In summer our table was laid in a clearing of the woods, sunlight or starlight dappling through the branches while the dogs sat hopefully at a respectful distance and the samovar hummed. Samovars are a salient feature of domestic life in Iran, as in Russia, and glasses of amber-coloured tea are drunk as constantly. I loved those meals, the patriarchal atmosphere and the family servants of two or three generations, who looked after us. They had poetic names, Moon-Fairy, or Jewel of Delight, and they spoke poetically. If I returned from a short walk they would say 'Your footsteps are on my eyes' or 'Your shadow has been missed' and if given an order, would reply 'May I be your sacrifice!' meaning, 'I will sacrifice myself to execute your order'. O! happy days when no one felt they lost caste by domestic labour, and no one's conscience pricked if they gave an order.

Yet even while I was rejoicing in those traditional ways – ways already remote from the West – progress in terms of modernisation was being pushed forward at an increasingly giddy pace. Every-where about the Turquoise Kingdom giant supermarkets were springing up, stacked with 'convenience' contraptions – deep freezes, push-carts, moving stairways, and tinned goods from faraway sources. Fewer and fewer of the small street-corner bakeries were to be seen about the expanding cities, and their excellent bread was giving place to cellophane-wrapped spongy white loaves obtained in chain-stores. They were the kind I used to see in America labelled 'factory fresh'; though there today, good bread is reinstated and home-made loaves are seen as a status symbol.

One of the charms of walking about Persian cities used to be the smell of freshly baked bread and the singular sight of those large dappled sheets of *sangak*, curiously spotted, dark and light brown, so that it seemed as if the population were always carrying a leopard-skin about with them.

Today, with a return both violent and mystical to all things traditional, no doubt the original dispossessed breads, like other local foods, are reinstated, while the tin-opener has become a symbol of Western degeneracy. It is a point of view hard to criticise.

That exquisite sense of design which is found in Persian carpets, like the intricate brick-work of the ancient mosques (I am remembering particularly the Friday Mosque at Isfahan) or the shimmering blue tiled work of a thousand other holy shrines, was also to be traced more simply in many other aspects of life. Even the presentation of some everyday dish echoed this profound, or atavistic sense of decoration. As in Japan, you might say. Certainly; but I will not embark on comparative niceties. Persian food, whether for a feast or daily life, was invariably pleasing to the eye by the manner in which it was presented. By that I do not imply all kinds of pretentious fiddlededee which swells out the *cuisine minceur* considered chic today. Rather a basic sense of display, and what best suited the material to hand, however modest. It is an Eastern trait.

Thus an encampment of the nomad tribes on the desolate plains beyond Shiraz, the Kashgai, let us say, would offer the plainest dish of rice – but it was no accident that it was piled into a huge bowl of coarse turquoise blue pottery. There would have been a white tin basin somewhere to hand no doubt, but that would spoil the effect of the snowy rice, and this they instinctively knew.

Shop windows, like booths in the bazaars, or along the streets, used to display ranks of pickle jars, and piles of melons or aubergines which recalled the intricate geometric patterns of a rug. Even the simple wooden spoons still in use (although many are now regarded as museum-pieces) were gracefully shaped, the best, called 'sherbet spoons', being of wafer-thin pear-wood, delicate as curved petals, had long stem-like handles perhaps eighteen or more inches in length. Such far-reaching spoons were strictly practical when everyone, from courtier to farmer or merchant, sat round on the floor and reached for one central dish; but a shorter form has remained, to grace the now more general Western-style table.

At those elaborate Persian banquets we see portrayed in miniatures, or that entrancing school of early nineteenth-century painting

known as Qadjar (from the dynasty of that name) the most voluptuous luxury is apparent. Thirty-seven courses were *de rigueur*, we
are told, and indeed, such largesse was maintained well on into the
twentieth century. Seventeenth-century travellers and diplomats
who succeeded in reaching the glittering Safavid court of Shah
Abbas at Isfahan were dumb-founded, for after many wearisome
months struggling across the barren wastes of Central Asia they
were confronted by unparalleled splendours. Their memoirs also
recorded a curious custom designed to refresh revellers at the Shah's
table. Between the courses, by way of diversion, a basket of kittens
(Persian of course) were often circulated, the guests fondling the
little creatures ecstatically. Cats were ever the Persians' especial
delight, and at the banquets they provided a kind of furry variation
to the customary undulating houris or their rivals, the painted
dancing boys. All of them were seen as a *détente* between the sumptuous sequence of gold, jewel-studded dishes the Shah, 'Allah's
Shadow on Earth', offered the assemblage crouched before him on
silken rugs beside pearl-tasselled bolsters.

Returning to a more modest scene, at the kind of Persian table I
once knew, a typical Persian dinner always began with *sabzi* (green)
which consists of tiny spring onions, chunks of cucumber, parsley,
mint and radishes. Every stratum of Persian society loves *sabzi,* and
I never noticed anyone had hiccups, or reeked of onions, so my
more queasy readers should take heart and put aside the heart-burn
mixtures and 'breathalators' of effete living.

Ashe is Persia's basic soup, a thick mixture of every imaginable
vegetable, and often accompanied by *köfte* – meat balls – heavily
spiced and marble sized. I came to know *ashe* well, when staying in
the province of Mazanderan in a house beside the curiously sullen,
greyish waters of the Caspian. There winter comes down early. An
incessant fine damp mist swirled mysteriously through the lush
groves of orange and mulberry trees, and then *ashe* came into its
own. We consumed it beside a fire of scented apple boughs, and as
the autumnal gales tore round the wood-tiled roof, blowing straight
in from the Russian steppes northwards across the Caspian, our
appetites were keen. In that house, the cook, a gifted boy from the
region, finding us enthusiastic, offered us a different kind of *ashe*
each of the six days we lingered there. In more southerly regions,
in great heat for example, there are cold versions, equally sustaining

but with yoghourt as a base. *Ashe* in one form or another has always been staple nourishment for the various peoples of Central Asia.

Rice, innumerable vegetables, fruit and yoghourt, or *mast*, are the country's staple diet. In many households, the main dish, or even the only one, was inevitably rice; but rice made intriguing by one of a series of intricate sauces – *khoresh* – either sweet or sour. These subtle but daring mixtures are the secret and the glory of traditional Persian cooking; as contradictory and complicated as the race itself. When deep in such delights as rice with *khoresh fesanjan*, I used to speculate as to its composition – the rice was transformed, the palate was stimulated ... what exactly were the ingredients? A small amount of meat, mixed with fruit and vegetables – but which? – were the basis of every *khoresh*. The stewy sort of sauce which resulted was transformed by such surprising additions as rhubarb or pomegranates, as in the case of *khoresh fesanjan*, or oranges, spinach and cinnamon, for *khoresh sak*. Such sauces might be described as the Persian equivalent of Italy's tomato-based accompaniment to pastas.

Chelo kebab is the quintessential Persian dish, found throughout the land, in private houses, wayside caravanserais, modern hotels or the small eating houses of the bazaars. *Chelo* is steamed rice, *kebab* grilled meat, and they are served with a sauce, which is something in the nature of a *coup de théâtre*. Beside each plate of rice and meat (lamb or beef) stands a raw egg in its shell, some powdered brown *sumak*, grated from the bark of the sumak tree, and a chunk of butter. But where is the sauce, you may ask? Where? – in its shell. You seized the egg (boldness and speed are essential to this operation) then, making a deep hole in the mound of rice, you cracked the egg open and stirred it into the rice along with the butter. All had to be done while the rice was blazing hot; a divinely rich yet simple sauce resulted, colouring the rice to a pale gold which was then sprinkled with the tawny sumak. The accompanying salad was invariably tomato and raw onion. I know of no better feast.

The Persian menu seldom included cheese as in so much of Europe and America. *Panir* was a very tough, very salty goat cheese, rustic in nature and eaten with melon or sprinkled with one of the innumerable spices of the Persian cuisine; it was also sometimes eaten with beetroot. In winter, cooked beetroot was sold smoking

hot from street barrows and whenever I was afoot in the swarming
bazaar quarter of Teheran (which I much preferred to the charac-
terless modern city), I found the beetroot a wonderfully sustaining
snack.

Apropos snacks, if so plebeian a phrase could be applied to caviar,
I always thought it ironic that the rare golden kind, reserved by
tradition for the Shah alone, was seldom served at the Palace, for
the monarch was allergic to caviar in any form; thus my curiosity
and the cravings of other guests were seldom fully gratified.

Persian deserts – *shirini* (or sweets), were not only extremely
sweet, but *très parfumés*. The puddings and tarts of our Western
world were not favoured. *Shirini* are lighter, a cross between honeyed
pastries and meringues, mostly flavoured with rose-water. A water-
ice of crushed mint, almost a sherbet, such as the sorbets we know,
was popular and called *sharbat*, but which was the original, sherbet,
or *sharbat*, who knows?

Fruit was abundant, of all kinds, while a certain small very delicate
cucumber ranked as such, and was eaten with sugar. Pomegranate
juice was drunk in large quantities for its health-giving properties,
much as we take orange juice. It was sold bottled, and gushed from
street soda-fountains, pressed and de-seeded, or was just cut open
and sucked noisily, messily, deliciously.

Finally, delicacy of all delicacies to me – there was *sekanjaban*, a
most elegant Persian extra, which I have never encountered anywhere but in Iran. This dish – though perhaps I should call it a
dip – first seduced me with its subtle, minty-sour sweetness, when
I encountered it at a picnic in the palm groves of an ancient royal
garden on the island of Kish (Sinbad's island according to legend),
a small sandy hump rising from the azure waters of the Persian
Gulf. Long spears of crisp Romaine lettuce were served with the
syrupy vinegar dip, and as I struggled to master the technique of
eating this elegantly, I thought that nursery bibs would have been
a practical accompaniment. This nation's innate sense of decoration
might have made each bib and tucker a work of art like tiles or
Kalamkar cotton prints.

When at last the picnic was over, and the sun sank behind the
snake-like limbs of the giant banyan trees, carpets were spread
beneath them, and we were invited to listen to the nightingales. In
the sultry dusk we waited, while I wondered how much of the
delicacy and elegance of this Persian feast I could transpose to my

own house. There, bamboo thickets, jacaranda, jasmine, cypress and fig replace the banyan. True, there are nightingales to sing for me, and carpets galore ... what then is missing? Simply this: my setting is the south of France – Europe ... and nothing can impose that curious ambiance, at once sophisticated and primitive, all age-old Asia, which makes up the arts and crafts, traditions and gastronomy of Persia.

CHAPTER 11

Eating for France
Diplomatic Dinners

For fifteen years of my life I was married to a French diplomat, which entailed a great deal of eating and drinking in the cause of international relations. The duties of a diplomat's wife are, basically, to represent her own country to the best of her ability, while following a curious contre-danse of protocol referred to as entertaining and being entertained (though this is often something of a misnomer for both states). A lot of store is set by keeping up with, or surpassing, the Joneses of other nations. Private means are of enormous help as allowances for entertaining are never enough. We did not have such means until my husband's books brought him fame – by which time he had decided to quit the career.

When I look back on those fifteen years, a chequer-board of luncheons, dinners, suppers and cocktail parties merge in a shimmer of cutlery, table silver and thousands of glasses. Moreover I seem to see them through that anguished haze of exhaustion known to every hostess remembering all the toiling and moiling that went on behind the scenes when preparing to 'entertain'. Almost as fraught were those struggles with small-talk (never politics) in the several languages required to break the ice at certain sticky international gatherings where one was, in turn, being 'entertained'.

Mostly, I remember the amount of eating that went on; we lived by a densely packed routine of complicated meals generally of a monotonous similarity, dishes composed of chicken or sole, chosen to avoid the religious or digestive problems of a multi-national corps. Thus a typical dinner would consist of consommé, sole or salmon mayonnaise, followed by a chicken dish with trimmings (no cheese and rarely a salad); and then the inevitable profiteroles, pêche melba or an iced *bombe*. And of course, a ritual *changement des vins* throughout, filling a covey of small glasses which were huddled beside our plates. After which, replete but scarcely vivacious we were shepherded back into a room where, probably, we had been regaled, only an hour or so earlier, with dry martinis, whisky, or champagne. Now came coffee and an array of death-dealing sickly pink and green liqueurs. Such an evening was taxing, following as so often a day which had included an elaborate luncheon, one or more cocktail parties or a National Day reception. It was thus that I came to describe my life as Eating for France.

Not such a bad life you will say, and I agree, for I lived it with reckless abandon, and no ill effects thanks to my uncomplaining liver. Moreover, at that time the pangs of conscience did not choke each mouthful, as they would today. All the horrors of Third World starvation, of dispossessed peoples and famines – the unsolved reality that is before our eyes now – were then a darkness lying ahead in some remote, unforeseen future.

One of the lesser-known obligations of a diplomat's wife was that round of calls known as *les visites*. At the time of which I write, in Berne, in particular, this exercise in etiquette was very strictly followed, for the Diplomatic Corps there observed the formal Spanish protocol. It had been drawn up centuries earlier and was only slowly falling into disuse elsewhere. One of its rulings entailed the doyenne of the corps (that is, the Ambassadress whose husband had been longest *en poste*) receiving the visits of all the newcoming wives at the various embassies. In turn, the doyenne presented them to the other Ambassadresses, in a round of fifteen-minute *visites* – with refreshments.

During my years in Berne, where my husband Romain Gary was First Secretary at the French Embassy, our dearly-loved Ambassadress was doyenne of the Diplomatic Corps and I was often detailed to accompany her on *les visites*. Perhaps this was because I spoke a little basic Russian, and could help out during the stickier silences that sometimes fell in Slavic circles. The Polish, Russian, Yugoslav or Bulgarian salons could prove quite a conversational challenge.

Punctually at four o'clock we would set out, hatted and gloved, with our card cases, and drive from house to house collecting the newcomers, whose cars would then follow ours. At the first port of call, the cortège would draw up, and the Ambassadress would lead the way into a drawing-room where a sister-Ambassadress awaited us. Seated in a rigid circle, we made as much polite conversation as the polyglot meeting permitted, while plied with refreshments. The doyenne was never so discourteous as to glance at her watch (she always claimed she had acquired a built-in time-clock) and after precisely fifteen minutes, she would pronounce the magic phrase, *Eh bien, mesdames* ... and with suitable expressions of regret we would rise, and follow her to further drawing-rooms and further expressions of international good will.

Although this stately *contre-danse* might seem removed from any questions of gastronomy, it was not so, for the refreshments customarily proffered were of a wildly varied nature, in striking contrast to the monotonous dinner tables already described. Indeed, they frequently led to hiccups and other digestive disorders, for according to each Embassy's expression of hospitality and a laudable wish to emphasise national delicacies, the callers might be offered, in the course of the afternoon, Turkish coffee, Swedish salted fish canapés, Romanian *ţuica* (plum brandy), frothy Mexican chocolate, cucumber sandwiches, Polish vodka, Christmas cake, tomato juice, milk-shakes or O! how welcome, China tea. Politesse demanded that all should be sampled even though *les visites* often followed a sumptuous luncheon and preceded a cocktail party which in turn led to a buffet supper.

The kitchens of our Embassy in Berne were under the maestro hand of a chef who had once been in the service of Queen Marie of Romania, and some note of Balkan exoticism (reflection perhaps of the Queen's own personality) was to be traced in the dishes he prepared. His pastry was richer and lighter, his sauces more seductive, his desserts more voluptuous than any others. And even when he produced a classic French buffet stand-by known as *le pain Louis XV* – de luxe ham sandwiches enclosed in a loaf – there was something especially succulent about his version. He never admitted to there being a secret ingredient; perhaps it was just the tidal waves of butter he used. They were ever his signature.

I like to think this delectable concoction originated at those hunting parties Louis XV held at Versailles or St Germain en Laye. They were a favourite subject for painters of the period – often portrayed as if in an elegant interior, where a white-wigged court quaffed and guzzled with stylish abandon, despite the plunging horses, dead game, hounds, grooms and lackeys surrounding the feast. Or, more aptly, Jean-François de Troy's simpler scene, *Le déjeuner de jambon*, another al fresco feast, beside a coach, in the shade of a country domaine – the *jambon* as its centre-piece.

Looking back, I have sometimes thought that had I led that kid-glove diplomatic life with a more conventional and efficient staff, and perhaps even another kind of husband, one more suited to social routines, I might have been less harassed. For a woman, much of diplomatic life depends not only on marital team work but the sort of servants she obtains. Our staff never were those pillars of discreet efficiency that by tradition, and on the screen, serve diplomatic households. Even when Chargé d'Affaires, Romain did not step into an embassy already replete with furniture and domestics – above all, a chef. Therefore, usually living in rented quarters, our servants were a motley lot, come-by-chance acquisitions, some of whom I loved, all of whom alternately exasperated and intrigued.

How bitterly I longed, sometimes, for a good plain French cook – not a chef – but one of those old-fashioned stalwart women from the provinces, born and bred to the traditions of a good bourgeois cuisine. For a short while I did obtain such a treasure, who, although looking strangely like an Aztec Shirley Temple, could roast, fry, bake, boil, and toil in the best manner. Then, boldly, I was able to offer my guests French country cooking. Regional dishes, *boeuf bourguignon, civet de lapin de Garonne,* or *choucroute alsacienne,* which they found an agreeable change from the usual diplomatic menus. But 'She was a good cook as cooks go, and as cooks go, she went', to quote Saki's immortal line.

Somehow, our budget never ran to menservants. Perhaps more regular ways might have prevailed then. As it was, hireling butlers or barmen helped out as the occasion demanded, always arriving at the eleventh hour and vanishing before the cleaning up began. (Oh! those vistas of glasses, all sizes and shapes, those leaning, Pisa-towers of plates!) At one point, our polyglot household consisted of a strangely compartmented staff, the cook, Russian, the gardener, Mexican, the cleaning man, Japanese, the secretary, Chinese-American, while the man who serviced the rather medieval electric installations was a pure-bred Sioux. Thus we never achieved that impeccable butlered style associated with a diplomatic household.

As to the place occupied by a *husband* in the life of a diplomatic wife – I can only speak of my own, who under no circumstances could be called representative. But then, as a couple, we were always labelled unorthodox – *writers* – rather odd, too, since neither of us were fired by the social ambitions which sustained many of our *chers collègues.* Although I did my best to present the façade which is so much part of diplomatic life, that was where our team-work broke down.

Romain could be marvellously entertaining, but ignored entertaining in the sense of attending to the needs of his guests. As he disliked alcohol, and seldom drank even wine himself, he made no effort to grasp essentials such as ice-cubes, or corks being replaced in bottles. I might find a startled guest clutching a whole tumbler-full of Cointreau, likewise, a parched late-arrival, panting for a long drink, might be given a sip or two of tonic water in a liqueur glass.

Another of his most trying habits during that kid-gloved gastronomic existence was to steal into the dining-room just before a dinner party and, seized by a sudden desire for fruit, help himself to some elegant table-decoration I had been at pains to devise – perhaps a huge water melon spilling over with tropical fruits and gardenias. Unaware of his deprivations, I would presently usher my guests towards the dining-room, only to be confronted with the demolished centre-piece.

In the countries to which we were posted, as in the lands we visited on our travels, I generally thought French hospitality ranked the highest gastronomically, which might be expected with France's age-old culinary traditions. Even in places where catering presented fearful difficulties, French know-how was apparent: though the atmosphere lacked a certain spontaneous warmth. As a nation, the French remain fiercely conventional. Thus you will be invited some considerable time ahead, and be offered their long-premeditated and perfected best. Pot-luck is eyed askance. An omelette would let the side down.

In France, when some glittering state banquet is given at the Elysée or Versailles, the menu will be published in detail, the public studying it with the same close attention a British public follows accounts of its Royal Family's weddings, confinements or christenings. I sometimes wonder if both nations are not, perhaps, expressly fed such detailed accounts as a means of distracting their attention from graver issues all around.

CHAPTER 12

In Memoriam : The East and West of the Romanian Table
A gastronomic fantasia

The Romanian cuisine is where you find it: that is, it varies as much as the climate and regions of this fascinating and multi-aspected land. Romania has snow, sledges, cruel winters *à la Russe*, and torrid, tropic summers. Thus Bucharest, the capital, swings between temperatures of Moscow and Madrid, and the blistering hot, long summers account for the enormous number of garden restaurants, *grădinăs*, which line the streets and spread far out into the countryside. It used to be the habit to dine very late, beginning around ten in the evening and sitting there into the small hours, sipping plum brandy, *tşuica*, listening entranced, seduced, spellbound – no adjective is too strong – to the traditional Romanian Gypsy music. This is akin to the better known Hungarian Gypsy music, but with an Oriental, or Turkish flavour added which makes it uniquely Romanian, both exotic and voluptuous. Nevertheless these *grădinăs* had a family flavour – plenty of children and grandparents too were ranged round the tables, and perhaps still are.

The overall Romanian cuisine is, like the race, a blend of Latin and Slav, with Oriental undertones. To give you some idea of what it was like to eat traditionally in Romania, we must cover a lot of ground – as I did, long ago, from the Carpathian mountains in the north, to the steamy southern waterways of the Delta, where the Danube flows into the Black Sea and the caviar fishermen catch and prepare this transcendental delicacy. Therefore, in order to achieve such a gigantic trajectory, let us suppose I can, by some magic, whisk your expectant taste buds, like your wide-open tourist's eyes, right across Romania, a supper here, a luncheon there ... sampling, briefly, the places and dishes I recall as being memorable.

Very well then: leaving nothing to chance and clutching our knives and forks, the quicker to be seated at table, we are off...! First, to one of the ancient fortified monasteries of the Bucovina, where the great painted frescoes now attract legions of tourists and art historians. When I knew them, and ate well there, some were convent communities of a special kind, now vanished. They were the retreat of certain privileged ladies, who occupied suites rather than cells, filled with their own elegant possessions, family pieces, books and portraits. Attended by humble novices they lived peacefully, did fine needlework, read widely, played the piano, gardened, made preserves, and attended matins and evensong (rather perfunctorily) to render thanks for so many blessings received. The atmosphere was less that of a religious order than of some eclectic, very aristocratic and cultivated club, presided over by the Abbess, who was my hostess and shall be ours now.

In the dim, white-washed and pillared refectory adorned with the inmates' family crests, we are seated at a long, polished wooden table, lit by heavy iron candlesticks. We sip *tşuica* and try some fiery little pimento pods dipped in yoghourt. Next, superb trout from a neighbouring mountain stream. Then, roast chicken with apricots, eaten of course with *mamaliga* (corn meal), for that is the staple dish – as national as *polenta* in Italy. There is also a side dish of mushrooms baked in sour cream. To follow, an extremely elaborate cake (of Turkish origin) called *catäif* (for which I have no recipe); composed of gauze-thin twists of pasta alternating with crushed walnuts and cinnamon, all drenched in a vanilla and honey sauce. No denials of the flesh here.

Looking round, between the courses, I am reminded of similar lay convents, equally indulgent, once spread about Denmark – a land which would seem by both character and situation very far removed from Romania. These Danish foundations for ladies of noble birth were of a rococo elegance bordering on frivolity and I had always wished to visit them. However, during the brief time I spent in Denmark (overcome by a sensational flight from Los Angeles via the polar route) I was too exhausted to do much more than eat fish and wander in the Tivoli gardens, where Hans Andersen still seems to linger. Entrancing as Copenhagen proved, the climate precluded expeditions to any of those distant estates of wind-blown farmlands and marshes where the convents are mostly situated. But my curiosity has simmered, ungratified ever since, cruelly fanned by descriptions with which Sacheverell Sitwell regaled me, recalling visits he made to them when writing his book on Denmark.

These convents were, like their Orthodox Romanian counterparts, prerogative of the *hoch-geböorn* – families with at least sixteen quarterings, and it was customary for the eldest unmarried daughter to become Abbess or Prioress of the Order. Eighteenth-century portraits displayed the ladies in full powder and diamonds, their mantles velvet or satin, lined with ermine, their ringed fingers holding some holy relic as nonchalantly as if it were a fan.

So, lingering in the rich but sober setting of this Romanian refectory, I realise how far apart are the two convents for noble ladies. This Orthodox setting is less sophisticated than its Lutheran counterpart. It has something of the sombre quietude of its surrounding forests, and reflects the austerity revealed in its ancient frescoed walls where the lay sisters are depicted as severe figures, long robed, in the Byzantine tradition. Nevertheless, in the refectory, a few naïve early nineteenth-century family portraits reveal later inmates, now as sophisticated as the Danish ladies, but with some added Oriental opulence emphasised by the sweep of their eyebrows, which join in that dark line once much cultivated by Turkish beauties. Even in this convent of Orthodoxy, a certain voluptuous idiom is traced. It recalls Turkish proximity and a not so distant past, when Romania was under Sultanate rule, and the Romanian princes or *hospodars* ruled *à la turque*, from cushioned divan thrones, smoking jewelled *tchibouks*, and wearing heavy brocaded caftans, their tall fur caps aigretted with jewels in the manner of a Sultan's turban. As to the ladies – though they did not go veiled, they were as exotic as any odalisque.

It was only during the middle and latter part of the nineteenth century, with the advent of a princely German ruler, that European ways were established, or imposed. Gradually, eastern flavours dwindled, leaving faint traces, however, still to be found at our next stop.

Now I am whisking you southwards to Bucharest, to one of the innumerable *grădinăs* where, under a trellised vine we shall choose a table which reveals a glimpse of the kitchens. There, the Gypsies are eating heartily before playing their intoxicating music for us, and a whole comedy of courtship is being conducted between the swarthy player of Pan pipes, and the peroxidey proprietress. These Gypsies are of the Lautari tribe, thieving, sensual, stealthy and irresistible. Again, we start off by sipping *ţuica*, then we try *mititei*, a porky sausage, grilled, and eaten with *mamaliga* on which a poached egg is posed. Now a superb pilaff of strongly saffron-flavoured rice with raisins, and crayfish. Next, a rabbity stew with prunes and paprika, a rustic dish, agreeable change after the more usual roast pork or lamb kebabs. We round off the feast with huge chunks of rosy melon, the melons being the most gigantic imaginable. All is washed down by local wines – not *grand cru*, maybe, but seeming nectar, when accompanied by the seducing rhythms of the Gypsies' music.

Music above all – Romanian music – those poignant, elusive *doîné*, the songs of the people, which 'steal our souls away'. Some are piercingly sweet, some savage: the Gypsy singers have a curious raucous tone recalling the *canto hondo* of Spanish gitanes. In any case, obsessive stuff. And so one eccentric music-lover found it, for, determined to share his raptures with uninitiated foreigners, he left a trust providing for a troupe of Gypsy musicians to be installed at a station where the earliest Orient Express used to halt – Giurgio, once the Serbian frontier, I was told. Thus passengers were both greeted and sped on their way by bursts of these furiously seductive strains.

Imagine this surprising scene. The monster engine steams to a halt and suddenly tawny faces and flashing eyes press close to the window – too close – grinning impudently.... Dark hands snatch, bare brown feet are seen capering round uniformed officials, or perched on piles of luggage with their violins, guitars and reed pipes, playing furiously, enticingly.... Did no passengers ever quit the train there and then – for ever – for such siren strains?

By now we have lost all count of time, lost a night's sleep, lost breakfast *en route*, and feel none the worse, as we suddenly find ourselves at Vâlcov, in the damp heat of the delta waterways and quite ready for a midday meal. Here the fisherfolk (many stemming from an old Russian exodus) are known as sea-Cossacks – Lippovans; they catch the Black Sea sturgeon for its caviar, living in primitive wooden huts raised on stilts above the marshy inlets. We, their guests, are seated around an equally primitive table, all dipping our wooden spoons into one huge, central bowl holding a succulent fish stew, composed of mixed-up chunks of the day's other catch, small fish, big fish, bits of sturgeon, fish liver, bones and all. This dish is the mainstay of such hardy folk. Not for them the luxurious salted caviar we may know – not yet the even more *de luxe* fresh, unsalted kind, an acquired taste, being curiously flat in flavour, and *very* oily. It used to be regarded as the supreme delicacy, but needed to be eaten within twenty-four hours, or it spoiled. Thus, rushed to the capital, it commanded exorbitant prices for *aficionados*. We do well enough without it now, however, sitting under the huge willow trees, every mouthful watched by the storks, pelicans and cormorants that abound here and approach for tidbits. Now we munch delicious, rather rough patties, or turnovers, made with the dark flour used for black bread. They are stuffed with chopped cabbage leaves, rice and a very salty bacon. *Mamaliga* again, of course, but now cut cake-like, very firm, with a dollop of buffalo-milk cream, and finally, enormous black grapes grown along the Black Sea shores, where the climate is Mediterranean.

Ehu fugaces! Those are the sort of menus I remember from long past Romanian days – where food, music and scene remain for me an indivisible, enticing mirage.

1. Breakfast in bed, if achieved, remains *the* sybaritic symbol, though today clouded by conscience. (Who'll carry the tray up how many stairs?) But the grandiose stairway at Carlton House aroused no such misgivings. Innumerable flunkeys remained undaunted before giddy heights and loaded trays. Theirs not to reason why.

2. In the *tchai-khana* or tea-house, two weary Afghans stack their rifles briefly, and savour the traditional solace of green tea spiced with cardamom.

The
Bua.també.

3. For this pair of frisky little Sumatra squirrels life is one long
picnic. Everything raw! and no washing up afterwards.

4. The sumptuous matron Kustodiev painted is doubtless a merchant's wife, and embodies the sort of nineteenth-century Russian provincial life that Gogol and Aksakov immortalised. The samovar hums, the cat purrs, and the summer evening sky reflects no coming storm.

5. Great Cairo as once.... The noonday repast is a man's world where the Patriarch regales his guests in cushioned ease attended by his household slaves. Doves flutter, roses scent the heavy air, and across the court, behind the fretted *mouchrabiyeh*, his harem peek and chatter and await his pleasure.

6. 'Step inside *effendi*! We have music, food, wine, and other
delights too,' cries the trousered charmer at this well stocked
but strangely empty Turkish *lokanta*. Could some more revellers
be temporarily occupied upstairs?

7. The quiet of the coffee-house is a timeless ritual across all Arab
lands. In desert tents or an emir's palace it remains unchanged
like the graceful form of the beaked coffee pots.

8. My kind of Christmas dinner table.

CHAPTER 13

Grand Food, Good Food and Grub

Grand food is not always good, nor is good food necessarily grand, while grub, so-called, the sausage and mash, jellied eel, shepherd's pie or pork pie plenty as once found in pubs, remains to me, at any rate, *hors* category – simply delicious. Grub (I do not know the etymology of the word) need not be a derogatory term unless applied to such horrors as technicolour pastries oozing imitation cream, or frozen fish fingers sloshed with ketchup. Once upon a time, really fresh fish used to be everywhere about our sea-girt isle. FRYING TONIGHT was chalked up outside the lowlier establishments and customers took away a packet wrapped in newspaper, hot, crisp, rather greasy and very good. It has been superseded in most places by more pretentious take-away stuff, just as traditional pub food has given place to pizzas or plates of pasta: the result, perhaps, of packaged Mediterranean holidays.

To define the exact category into which the different dishes fall is tricky. Often, they overlap, or are borderline cases, one being elevated by the manner in which it is prepared, while another is degraded. A rack of lamb with mint sauce is, to my mind, grand food: yet Alexandre Dumas' *gigot de sept heures* is probably considered far more grand, by its reputation, if not its complication. A *soufflé aux oeufs mollets* sounds grand. Yet it is, in fact, only soft boiled eggs popped into a soufflé at the crucial moment. What puts it into a top category is knowing how and when to get the eggs into the soufflé. Legerdemain as well as ingredients count here.

A pudding of undisputed grandeur and pomposity is the Byculla Soufflé, invented by the Byculla Club of Bombay. It was the sort of thing Simla hostesses aspired to when out to dazzle; there may still be some very old ladies who can recall its multi-coloured layers of *mousse*, green Chartreuse, yellow Bénédictine and crimson Maraschino. That is grandeur – though not necessarily goodness.

Flamboyance of that order would not be found at the tables of such acknowledged epicures as the Rothschild dynasty *en bloc*, or at the table of that prince of bankers and epicures, the late Pierre David Weill. In that exclusive coterie of top French chefs – those who *choose* their employers rather than being chosen by them – Monsieur David Weill ranked above almost every other *fine fourchette* (literally, 'a delicate fork'), which somehow promises a more appreciative approach than our 'good trencherman'.

This specialised world of aesthetic gastronomy, which in France does still exist, though diminished, was encouraged during the presidency of Monsieur Giscard d'Estaing, another *fine fourchette* who had the Elysée humming with chefs, or *toques* as they are known, after the high pleated caps of their profession. (*'C'est à table qu'on gouverne'*, as Bossuet remarked.) These *toques*, or *gros bonnets* as they are also called, are pundits, who stand no nonsense from any dilettante employer. There must be no nerve-racking sudden change of menus planned some days ahead. They, like those who can afford to pay them, and the feasts they concoct, live in a very rarified atmosphere.

My life in Paris and New York sometimes gave me glimpses of this world when I dined with Pierre David Weill or *chez* Elie de Rothschild. However, once inside the latter's historic house in the seventh arondissement (a quarter, where between the embassies and other historic houses, the thickest concentration of chefs is found) the Baronne's extraordinary collection of pictures, furniture and bibelots once belonging to Queen Marie-Antoinette quite distracted me from my plate. But while below stairs the chef and his *marmitons* were conjuring up masterpieces, a lively and critical interest was maintained upstairs. A dish which I took to be perfection, the Baron Elie might pronounce as middling.

There can be no family with more great dishes named after them than the Rothschilds, and their initiation into the subtleties of gourmandise, begun early, is always developed by their close association with the great chefs they employ. I remember the Baron Elie told me he was brought up, like his brothers and cousins, to take the art of cooking seriously. As a schoolboy, his weekly half-day holidays were largely spent in the kitchens learning the rudiments of gastronomy from the chef. Tuition began at the beginning – how to boil an egg, and so on, to higher flights.

The disciplines of the *haute cuisine* did not quench the boy's enthusiasm, nor did the rigid niceties of wine tasting, of forming the palate, as imposed by the butler. There is a story, perhaps apocryphal and attributed, I think, to Alan Pryce-Jones, which I beg leave to quote. It goes something like this: on entering a Rothschild nursery to fetch his little son who was partying there, he observed one of the children fidgeting to get down. 'Not till you have finished your Château Lafite', said Nanny.

In Paris I sometimes dined with the Windsors, another house where the finer shades of gastronomy were perfectly expressed. The menus the Duchess composed were never banal; she boldly mixed simple and sophisticated food, thus tickling the most jaded palate. Countrified dishes and local fare such as a *cassoulet*, or a *navarin printanier* were found at her beautiful table, where she might mix rustic pottery with a service of vermeil. Subtle oriental sauces, Mexican black-eyed peas or the homely spud baked in its jacket were enjoyed there, as well as the classic French cuisine at its finest. The Duchess's knowledge was held in high respect by the critical circle of Paris chefs. 'She was the perfect *patron*' was their verdict. The Duke, who sometimes disturbed his chefs' Olympian calm by asking for a sandwich at some unlikely hour, used to speak fervently of typical English food, York ham, crumpets or Gentleman's Relish and once told me he had retained some aged servitor solely for the way in which he cooked the Duke's breakfast bacon.

I suppose I shall now receive spiteful letters from some of the Duke's detractors: but as the saying goes, I speak as I find, and I remember many delightful times with the Windsors, enjoying both their company and their table.

I have not written of Indian food here, nor of my travels in that fabled land. The fiery cuisine caused me suffering too strong for any recollection in tranquillity. I do remember, however, an occasion when our car drew up before a wayside gas station which advertised Snacks. The proprietor rushed out and, thrusting a smiling turbanned head in at the window, enquired 'Memsahib, stopping for a snake?' And at that moment, in the molten heat, my mouth still blistered from the last curry, I could have relished a nice cool slice of cobra.

The most dismal meal I ever faced – grub at its lowest denomination, was on a Red Indian reservation set high on a desolate, wind-bitten *mesa* or table-land on the Arizona and Nevada border. These were Hopi Indians, a tribe not quite so dramatic or terrifying as the Sioux or Comanches, the kind with whom I was familiar through a life-long passion for Westerns – still, Redskins.

The Hopi were aloof, if not hostile to the outside world of pale-faces; they were not the more gregarious lot who paraded and performed their war dances for the annual tourist jamboree at Flagstaff. Only the good offices of a Mexican friend who was *persona grata* among these Hopi, had secured my invitation, so I set off in a ferment of ethnological enthusiasm. The long rough drive was a trial for both my small car and myself, while the case of whisky I had been advised would be an acceptable gift shifted ominously in the boot as we bucketed about the rock-strewn track – I was to stay the night on the reservation, and the further I drove into the remote distances the less I liked the idea.

On reaching the *mesa*-top, all was desolation: a huddle of shacks and lean-to sheds, a dipper well, with a decrepit mule tethered to it, and a bricked-up structure, once the school-house, I learned later, which had been imposed by the US government and soon rejected. In the shelter of a rock ledge, a flint faced gaffer was carving one of those sinister Katchina doll-figures now regarded as museum pieces. There was no other sign of life. Where were the tepees – the braves, the mustangs? A vicious wind raged round and tumbleweed shifted to and fro aimlessly. It was high time for a whisky.

Presently a bundled-up group of beady-eyed matrons waddled towards me – squaws – the real thing, and a monosyllabic lot; but at last I understood that an important festival was about to begin, something to do with invoking the rain gods, though perhaps I got it wrong for a heavy drizzle was now falling before it had been invoked. The squaws led me to a deep pit and I climbed down a shaky ladder to where, in the middle of the pit, a large fire smoked uncomfortably as the rain hissed down. Circling the fire were a number of men – the braves at last! Impassively, they were per-forming a curious ritual dance, hopping, capering and grunting rhythmically. Some wore blue jeans: all were hung with strips of coloured cloth, and little bells, thus bearing a fatal resemblance to Morris dancers.

The ceremony was still going on some hours later when the

squaws summoned me to the surface, pantomiming a meal. A real Red Indian meal? Strips of dried buffalo? Some aromatic stew of deer meat? But it was not to be. With a generous hospitality they could ill afford, the Hopi had sent one of their younger men to the nearest village store many miles away, for the sort of thing the pale-faces ate. *He* knew. *He* had been a corporal in the US army and his purchases were now spread before me in triumph. 'Convenience foods' in all their ghastly variety. Beefburgers, hamburgers, cheeseburgers and Mother's Bake deep freeze apple pie. All were frozen rock hard . . . . Several hours were now spent thawing them over a fitful fire, or, in desperation, burying them among the embers. It was nightfall when at last I could start on a few chips of Mother's Bake pie. The rest of the company had long since devoured some kind of delicious-looking corn mush which, although hot, was not for me, the pale-face. So much for grub, Hopi or supermarket style.

When I returned to Hollywood, where my husband and I were then living, an affluent society was in full fling all around. I have often been asked since what the film stars ate, what sort of parties they gave and so on. The stars' first consideration was inevitably their weight, and their usual menu grills, salads and fat-free milk. Poor souls. The big studios, MGM, Warner Bros or Universal provided cafeterias where I often ate during a later, happy time when I was working for George Cukor at MGM. In these cafeterias everyone from star to technician could be found though some stars preferred to eat – or drink – in their dressing rooms. Alcohol was not obtainable at the cafeterias. But the most hallucinatory salads abounded, cottage cheese with pieces of lettuce, banana, and a cherry or two imprisoned in green jelly. These and other equally odd combinations were named after various stars. Thus an order would ring out for 'Elizabeth Taylor on rye', or 'Gary Cooper sunny side up with pecan pie'. Enormous almost raw Texan steaks were popular – macho food for macho men. Yet, curiously, puddings seemed to lose all control, weight-wise, and were baroque structures, jumbo sundaes and milk shakes.

In their sumptuous houses at Bel Air or Beverly Hills, the inner circle of success, top stars, directors, producers and agents entertained each other lavishly, usually on Saturday nights, when there was no brooding shadow of a five a.m. studio-call to which the stars were liable, since it often required three or four hours of being made up, dressed and prepared for the camera by eight a.m. Sometimes there were Sunday lunches round the pool when the host worked hard at a smoking barbecue, and occasionally wore a chef's cap. Dinners in this society were luxurious, conventional, and very good. The living was high – the best of everything along with the latest styles of interior decorating. Cooks were usually Europeans, French for preference, or at any rate were cooks of some style, like the butlers, who were prized especially if British.

After dinner, the pattern was generally the same. Replete and sunk in voluptuously padded armchairs we sipped our coffee and liqueurs and waited while the walls – invariably hung at that time with French Impressionists (genuine, if not always Grade A) – slowly folded back giving place to a large screen which treated us to the newest preview, or maybe some Golden Oldie starring our hostess in her prime. There was always a lot of ribald comment and chaff, besides chilling silences. This was an audience of critical professionals. Yet there was something cosy, an almost family atmosphere in the Hollywood I knew in the 'fifties. Those were the last years before television took over; the Hollywood of directors such as John Ford, George Cukor and David Selznick, and stars such as Marlon Brando, Marilyn Monroe, Gary Cooper, Charles Boyer and John Wayne, with high-powered agents such as Charlie Feldman and Swifty Lazar who manœvred them. Kirk Douglas was on the way up, and the young Paul Newman was being tipped for a big future. Kate Hepburn, who lived in a bungalow at the end of George Cukor's garden, always refused to attend his dinners (the best of all, sparked by his outrageous, extravagant wit and sophisticated taste). But Miss Hepburn abhorred dressing up as much as social life – though she sometimes sneaked up to the kitchens, a shadowy figure in blue jeans, to pick over the delicacies, unrebuked by cook or host.

But before I take leave of Hollywood, where good food was *de rigueur*, if not in the grandest category, I am reminded of one of the most perfect dinners I have ever known, in Hollywood or elsewhere. Cole Porter was the host, and Fred Astaire was the only other guest beside my husband and myself. The menu? Caviar, followed by pheasant and a soufflé Grand Marnier. Grand food, in the grandest company. And if in this chapter I have appeared to be name-dropping, what else can I do? Were I to write: 'Dinner with C.P. and F.A.', even such food would lose some of its lustre.

I had better get back to nameless company and grub – the best sort – which is, essentially, ever my choice, to be sought with the zeal of a truffle hunter. As I have remarked earlier, this is traditional English food and for all my life of travel, of pilaffs, kebabs and fricassees, I love best suet pud., bangers and toad-in-the hole. ... When I return occasionally to London, and sight one of those small chalet-like green structures, the cab-man's shelter (unique, I believe to London streets), I stand transfixed, sniffing the heady wafts of boiled beef and cabbage or Irish stew and dumplings simmering within, hot and plentiful, awaiting the fortunate taxi-man and his appetite.

Yet even as I assert my preference for grub, I am contradicted by a faraway memory. Some un-nameable exotic aroma rises round me. It overcomes the homely wafts of cabbage, for it is the cuisine of Byzantium I am remembering. I have written of this elsewhere but to recall such historic grandeur seems fitting here.

Long ago I was staying in a country house at Rhinebeck up the Hudson River. Each night I tasted food which aroused my curiosity to fever pitch. Such food was unlike anything I had ever eaten – and far more exquisite. Although the ingredients were recognisable, there was some subtle opulence, some exoticism which baffled me. It was a cuisine of immense intricacy, yet bold: Asiatic, rather than Arab, I thought. It was certainly *haute cuisine*, yet mysteriously spiced and treated. 'Ah! that is Vassili's secret' said my hostess.

Vassili was her old chef and had been with the Obolenskys since they fled from Russia during the revolution. He had begun as one of the hundreds of *marmitons* at the Winter Palace, and also served in the kitchens of the Grand Duke Vladimir's palace. The Romanoff Court maintained certain archaic rituals which were handed down like certain culinary traditions, an almost unbroken line stemming originally from the Byzantine court of Constantinople. They had reached Russia along with the first roses and that double-headed eagle, symbol of Byzantine sovereignty which was adopted by Russia, when the Paleologi princess Zöe journeyed north to become the Tsarina Sophia, wife of Ivan III. Thus even the faintest echoes of Byzantine grandeur must take pride of place over any other cuisine, in these pages.

CHAPTER 14

Nile-side Meals

Egyptian menus are apt to read like a list of feminine charms, and arouse the most voluptuous imaginings .... Ladies in a Mosquito Net, *fisolis*, is a kind of luscious fruit latticed with crystallised sugar; *kadin budu*, or Ladies' Thighs are plump little rissoles (as popular in Turkey as in Egypt); Ladies' Fingers are *bamyias,* which we know as okra; *oum Ali* – the mother of Ali – is a cake composed of the most diaphanous layers of pastry, with almonds and cream; *soriti sitt* – Ladies' Navel – is a kind of *petit four,* a circular whorl, naturally, and particularly favoured by the sweet-toothed Egyptian men who gather under the heavy-scented limes or acacia trees at dusk.

As a whole, Egyptians live frugally: the more elaborate concoctions are found in big towns, produced for festive occasions or in sophisticated households. They are generally a legacy from those detested centuries of Turkish domination. The *fellahin* – peasants – and country people still eat much as their ancestors of ancient Egypt did (the pyramids were said to be built on a diet of bread and onions). Their food today is largely vegetables, corn, dates, buffalo cheese, goat flesh and Nile fish. Pistachio nuts are used here in the place of the almonds found in other Middle Eastern dishes. They are held to be a sovereign remedy against liver ailments, and are used in both meat and sweet concoctions, some of which, to the Western palate, appear fantastically over-imaginative.

Alas! All over the Middle East, and the Orient too, many hotels only provide mangled versions of a Western cuisine, imagining this satisfies and reassures their visitors. But people travel to see other countries, other ways: local colour should include the *best* local cuisine. Ministries of tourism, travel departments and chefs should take heed: in particular, I am addressing here two historic Egyptian hotels I know and love above most other caravanserais –Shepheard's in Cairo, and the old Winter Palace at Luxor. Both have long traditions of perfection in every other aspect – perfect service, perfect comfort, and each is incomparably placed, overlooking the Nile as do many new towering hotels. If only they would indulge their guests further by examples of the national cuisine: after all, we do not come to Egypt to eat bacon and eggs, or jam tarts.

However, it must be admitted that for more than a century, thousands of Europeans reached Egypt or the Middle East clamouring for just such familiar foods. Before the Suez Canal opened the way to India, the cruel overland route passed through Cairo and there was only Mr Shepheard's hotel to cater for the British Army officers and their wives, or those travellers and traders who shuttled back and forth, dust-covered pallid figures sheltered by pith helmets or dark veils, always clasping stomach mixtures and insecticides – though neither of these was needed by those who put up at Shepheard's.

The apogee of both Shepheard's and the Winter Palace was probably reached during the later, palmy Edwardian days so well described in Robert Hitchen's novel *Bella Donna*. Time seemed to stand still for the privileged, then. Certainly for the English, there to administer Egypt under Lord Cromer's governorship. He controlled diplomatic and domestic issues, while Field-Marshal Lord Kitchener's troops ensured order; the seething Egyptian patriots had not yet boiled over. Then, for rich travellers, to winter in Egypt was the chic thing to do. A whole world of international aristocracy, high finance, sharping riff-raff, polo playing oriental princes, fine ladies, or those of the Parisian demi-monde and their protectors were to be seen on the terrace at Shepheard's, while another kind of spectacle, that of Cairo's Ezbekieh Square, was unfolded below – trotting donkeys, lounging *fellahin*, little spanking carriages, beggars and veiled women.

At Luxor, in Upper Egypt, yet another kind of spectacle was unfolded. Rural Egypt, an abiding scene of Nile-side life and the river's legendary afterglow were both to be observed from the crimson balustraded balconies of the old Winter Palace (now made over and enlarged but still balconied). There, in those days, before speed-boats and sun-tan, the same luxurious crowd, slightly leavened by archaeologists busy with the tombs of the Pharaohs, all congregated to marvel and exclaim. As the sun dropped behind the tawny Libyan mountains and the great river faded from a rosy sheen to silver, then greenish pearl, and at last, in a flood of reflected brilliance, shimmered to a golden afterglow which slowly sank to dusk, then even the most mundane chatter was hushed, briefly, as darkness fell and the ladies clapped their kid-gloved hands – gloved, even in Eden. And then, collecting their ostrich-plumed fans and feathered boas and cigar-smoking escorts, they swept into the restaurant where, to the strains of an Australian orchestra playing the 'Blue Danube' (really more their sort of river than the Nile) the *maître d'hôtel* proposed *sole véronique,* roast beef and *Sacherorte*, just the kind of international hodge-podge I have condemned for being out of place – of having no relation to the *genius loci*.

There is no doubt that it is how a dish is first eaten that casts its spell for good, or ill. Thus the pleasantest food, coinciding with a liver attack, will never regain its prestige, while dry husks will seem a soufflé under certain circumstances. I recall, longingly, some breakfasts in Upper Egypt where, before the great heat beat down, I drifted in a felucca, eating odd-looking Nile fish stewed with vegetables and numbers of unknown herbs, washed down by the sticky-dark sweet tea much favoured thereabouts. *This* food, served *there* appeared perfection – it belonged: though fish so cooked would be good elsewhere (if not for breakfast). I think it was simmered in sesame oil, with okra, red peppers, onions and little marrows, which provided a mushy sauce. I never saw it cooking, since the mother of Kamal, my boatman, used to prepare it for us and bring it down, fuming hot, to the water's edge below the palm-grove village where she lived with her eleven other sons. She was a majestic matriarch, stepping proudly, while behind her, a yard or more of fringed aubergine-coloured drapery trailed in the sand. This was no careless abandon but the custom of the women thereabouts, designed to sweep away their footprints, the better to fox Chäitan – Satan, the Devil himself, were he following them.

My knowledge and appreciation of the Egyptian cuisine has come from many unexpected quarters – from the hospitality of government officials, a religious leader, exiled Caucasians settled in Cairo, musicians, architects and journalists. Among the most cherished sources, another wonderful matriarchal figure, equally massive, with the huge painted eyes of an idol. She had long been treated as such, for she had been the most celebrated of belly-dancers from Cairo to

Alexandria. In her old age she was still considered the finest teacher of that undulating art which in its purest form stems from the temple rituals of ancient Egypt. She was also an excellent cook, delighting to pass on as many kitchen tips as I demanded. But first, something about her profession.

It had been my good fortune to gain her friendship through my interest in the tradition behind this vanishing art – for so she saw it and so it seemed to me, nourished on descriptions of those serpentine charmers, the *gazeeyahs*, a tribal class of dancing girls peculiar to old Cairo. The dancing boys, as painted, as alluring, were called *khäwals*, and Edward Lane has described these singers and dancers in his classic *Manners and Customs of the Ancient Egyptians*. If any of such traditional performances remain they are generally in a debased form, night-club stuff which the old lady deplored loudly, telling me of her early days, and of the great dancers from whom she learned her art. This fabled band of earlier seductresses spanned the centuries, a living chain of flesh, high priestesses of all desires. Our conversations were generally conducted in her hideous modern apartment, over a luncheon table loaded with steaming casseroles, pickled fish, and a cherished tin of Everton's toffee. After lunch, the six-piece set of gilded armchairs, a gigantic buffet adorned with paper flowers and the massive table were pushed around to make room for the classes about to begin.

A succession of young Egyptian girls appeared, stripped to a brassière, with a gauze rag tied low on their hips. They were plump, but in no way the full-moon houris of Eastern lore. Their beautiful, soft, dark faces were grave as they concentrated, postured, writhed, writhed again, advanced and retreated with small, sipping steps, a pantomime of seduction which the old teacher mimed with them, corrected sharply, or praised. Some of her pupils were already star performers, returning for a refresher course. Some girls had brought their families to watch, and a number of persons ranging from a four-year-old (who joined in) to toothless crones, husbands or lovers, all peered through a beadhung *portière*, leading to the kitchen where a Nubian woman was making lemonade for the gathering between dashes to wind up an antique gramophone. Everyone seemed aware of the sacred elements which the old teacher upheld. These were no ordinary dancing classes. 'The belly movements – the hips – all that can be learned easily enough,' said my hostess, sucking a piece of toffee noisily. 'It is by the hands, the language of

the hands and arms that *real* style is seen.' As I watched the beckon-
ing, delicately curled fingers and the shuddering snake-like arms of
a star pupil, my surroundings faded .... I saw the painted *ghazeeyehs*
posturing before Bonaparte's victorious generals, in striped tents
beside the Pyramids .... I saw the beautiful Temple of Hâthor at
Dendérah ... Hâthor, the Goddess of Love, whom such dances
have honoured through the ages ....

'If you come back tomorrow I will make you *sitt alnoubéh*,'
said my hostess, who had noticed that my appetite for traditional
Egyptian food was as keen as my appreciation of her art. *Sitt
alnoubéh* – the Nubian woman – takes its name from its dark colour,
and is, I think, a sweet chicken stew, with purslane and pastilles of
aloe... but I would not like to be quoted on that ... (*very* Wilder
Shores, as my friends would say).

A typical good Egyptian meal, such as you would find in any private
house, or a modest little restaurant, might begin with *meloukhia*, an
opaque, purée-like green soup, made from jews' mallow, *mauve des
juifs*. Another starter might be *taheena*, that rich mixture of hummus
(chick-peas) worked to a suave cream with sesame oil. This is to be
found tinned in many exotic delicatessen stores. Thinned, drop by
drop, with water, it makes a perfectly irresistible substance in which
to dunk pieces of that flat unleavened bread eaten all over the Middle
East. At home I have tried a geographic mix-up by substituting
fingers of grilled Pumpernickel, as black as the forest of its Germanic
origin. Another Egyptian starter, though often the peasants' main
dish, is *foul*, dried beans soaked overnight and cooked with oil, and
eaten with fresh lime juice. With hard boiled eggs, it becomes more
interesting. Tomatoes transform it into a salad.

Egyptian fish dishes are predominantly Mediterranean in style,
the best being the specialities of Alexandria. Sometimes a large fish,
such as bass, sword-fish or tunny will be stuffed with onions, parsley
and herbs, and smothered in *taheena*, that same rich sesame sauce
which I have just described. This dish, known as *musayadiya*, can be
eaten hot or cold.

The main course might be lamb kebab, or pigeon stewed with
vegetables. In Cairo there are pigeon restaurants which serve
nothing else, but the variety is infinite. Vine leaves, or aubergine
stuffed with a sour-milk cheese are among the best vegetarian dishes.
Foul medammess are croquettes of puréed brown beans or lentils,

often served as an accompaniment to meat; they are, like most Egyptian foods, strongly spiced. Yet how to describe, or evoke here, those dominant yet subtle wafts of unnameable and probably unobtainable spices which rise from the plate, or drift about one's memory, as one recalls the bazaar restaurants or street booths of Cairo? I can only advise a boldly imaginative use of any spices to hand to make (or mar) the whole.

To continue the meal, which is always a lingering affair, a salad of tomato and onion pickle, or undressed lettuce will follow the main dish; the classic vinaigrette is unknown here, like mayonnaise.

For pudding, there will be *melahabiyeh*, a scented ground rice, or one of those intricate cakes, dripping honey. Fruit, figs, melons, grapes and dates are served, depending on the season, while tea has superseded coffee in popularity, to round off the meal. This is always drunk from little glasses and in winter it is sometimes laced with ginger, which is particularly comforting and a practice I have adopted at home. No milk, of course, but often some exotic jam, coconut or bitter orange will be offered alongside as a *bonne bouche*.

All kinds of sophisticated sherbets or water ices are favoured by this race so delicately attuned to the nuances of living, and they are still, in some houses, served in enchanting little glass or porcelain-lidded cups, called *kulleh* – collector's pieces today. These sherbets are full of surprises, for while a lemon sherbet will be lemon coloured, there is one, particularly esteemed, made from crystallised violets which is, oddly, green, and I have been told of a liquorice sherbet which is a sickly pink – one of the rare Egyptian delicacies I do not crave; liquorice is damned forever in my eyes, having been the mainstay of that ghastly mixture known as liquorice powder, Nanny's invariable revenge when I had overeaten or as she called it 'looked peaky' (though one looked a lot more peaky after being dosed with the liquorice mixture). Thus, can the long shadows of childhood return to cast a blight over even the most radiant Egyptian dinner-table.

CHAPTER 15

The Hubbard Cupboard
Emergency Dishes from Small Nothings

Suddenly, unexpected friends appear and have to be fed. It is too late to make a dash to the shops. (Of course this crisis would not arise in the USA where there is always some supermarket somewhere that stays open throughout the whole night.) A frantic survey of the refrigerator increases your panic, while your store cupboard badly needs replenishing, a state of affairs you have neglected to put right. Nevertheless, it is not quite so bare as old Mother Hubbard's. You have, let us say, rice, anchovy essence, or a small jar of anchovy fillets. There are still one or two eggs in the fridge – though not enough for the standby omelette – and there is a sprig of parsley in the windowbox. So you can produce a *kind* of kedgeree. 'Kind of' is the operative phrase in such cases, for it stifles criticism.

Apropos store-cupboard essentials. I was once discussing the subject with the late James Beard, doyen of American cookery pundits. We were in my garden, sitting under an avocado tree, after a lunch which my guests seemed to have enjoyed, if second helpings do not lie. The question arose: if we were limited to only three extras or added ingredients, the basic food apart, what would they be (salt not counted)? Which three *flavourings* would see you through; which three would you choose with which to test your inventive skills on menus which covered salads, fish, meat and sweets? With hardly any hesitation, we settled for onions, lemons and honey. Onions, of course, for being more versatile than garlic and generally more acceptable too. Onions enliven fish, meat and game. Onions are often the hidden ingredient of a good soup, and rubbed round the salad bowl, are substitutes for garlic. Lemons are for almost everything – in all vegetable soups, as salad dressing and in most fish dishes; with most poultry too. Stuff a chicken with half a lemon, rub the bird over with the other half, and enjoy the delicate, light

99

flavour this gives. Honey, a natural sugar, needs no explanation. It too, can be allied to meat and poultry. A roast of pork, like a roast chicken, browns in a more succulent fashion if rubbed over with honey, and a salad dressed with lemon and a trace of honey is excellent.

Thus, these three basic flavourings can, *à la rigueur*, replace a whole store cupboard of this and that.

Spaghetti seems to be the most popular of last resorts. There is little thought or invention when it comes to the standby spud. Yet what versatility that humble tuber displays when removed from the mash, chip or crisps monotony. Kitchens beyond the perimeter of easy-living have always given the potato pride of place, since there were no rich dishes which merely required it as an accompaniment. There is the Irish 'champ' and 'colcannon' where the potato demands some green vegetable, leeks or cabbage to help it out. There are Jewish *latké* which only need eggs beside; the Bulgarian *musaka kartofi*, a potato pie, only asks for a little onion and tomato; the Scottish 'rumbledethumps', like 'colcannon', has potatoes and green vegetables together; but the potato dominates in all of them.

Such dishes are sturdy; they evoke the smell of peat smoke, moorland air or the salt tang of the Donegal coast. But *latké* is something else. Its name alone conjures dim, cellar-like dwellings, candlelight and poverty – the medieval ghettoes of central and eastern Europe. Eating *latké* I am again in Prague, long long before the holocaust, and the powerful magic of that city envelopes me in a strange miasma of Jewish legend.

I had been wandering, all day, about the beautiful old streets returning fascinated to the historic ghetto, with its age-old synagogues, the Pinkas, or the 'new–old', and the crumbling burial ground where all the sombre legends and mysticisms of the Hebrew past press round; the Golem, and Uriel Acosta, the Rabbi Loew and the Student of Prague were all jumbled in my head as I crossed the statued bridge and wandered fearfully, between huddled walls, in the Street of the Necromancers: Mozart had lived in the light, above, at Betramka . . . . They were giving the 'Jupiter' at the City Hall that night, but then I remembered I wanted at all costs to see the Habima Players' performance of *Dybbuk*, that most terrifying of all Jewish legends. Such legends still cast a sinister, *unheimlich* spell about much of Prague and it seemed fitting to look for some simple, old-fashioned restaurant serving traditional Jewish food. (This was long before I lived in New York where there would have been no need to search.) Thus, at last, in a dim, tunnel-like café, I came to *latké*, which has remained a favourite potato dish for me, in my Goy kitchen.

But back to shortages, to emergency dishes, with and without potatoes, always assuming that your cupboard has, even in its shamed state, some elderly onions, some rice, or polenta, the remains of a tube of tomato purée, the scrapings of a jar of marmalade, stale biscuits and such, the sort of odds and ends which lie about waiting to be thrown out. That is, unless they can be incorporated into some of the recipes on p.164 and so avert a crisis.

CHAPTER 16

Arabian Aromas

Everywhere in Arab lands from Jordan to the Saudi-Arabian ports along the Red Sea and the lavish Gulf Emirates, food is very highly spiced – but it is a quite different gamut of spices to those of India – or so it has always seemed to me. In each town, or village *souk*, the spice booths are fascinating and magnetic – my first port of call. Mysterious powdered substances overflow big sacks and are scooped out by the pound, unlike the midget-stoppered jars of this and that to which we are accustomed. Nor do these great open landslides of spices, dusty brown, violet, yellow, green or orange, seem to lose their potency, thus exposed. In Oman, along the enchanting waterfront of Muscat, the lacy white fretted balconies of the old houses and all the alley-ways swim in heady odours wafted from the nearby spice bazaar. In the blue bay, sheltered by a sharp-cragged coastline, amongst all the turmoil of a modern port there are still some of those curiously formed high-pooped wooden craft such as the *baghala* or *gangha*, age-old pride of the Omani ship-builders at Sohar. Such craft will have returned from Zanzibar – the spice island of legend – with an entire cargo of cloves. Such is the demand, hereabouts.

Throughout these Arab lands rice is a staple: mutton and goat are roasted and fish is sometimes cooked with sesame oil, crushed mint or coriander. Surprisingly, dried fruits, fresh gooseberries, or plums also accompany fish. For a feast, *mechaoui* remains the classic dish. For this, a sheep is roasted whole, and often stuffed with raisins, rice and pistachio nuts, along with such spices as the cook, and tradition, demands.

Pigeon is the chicken of the desert and best cooked *en casserole*, or in one of those earthen dishes which come to table under a tall dunce-cap cover. In Morocco they are known as *tajeen*, where they are often made of chased silver – very stylish. A pigeon stew with prunes is one of Morocco's classic dishes, served in a *tajeen*; another is lamb, with quince.

In the deserts of the Middle East where one is often on short commons, the Bedouin will at once offer to kill a goat to celebrate your arrival; hospitality demands no less. If you can avoid causing this slaughter, you may be very well fed on some impromptu snack. Perhaps a treacly mass of dates and a bowl of creamy curds or slices of hard white goat's cheese fried in oil. Eaten hot, with a handful of black olives, a round of Arab bread added, this is a most satisfying snack.

Meza are the appetisers with which every Arab meal begins, an unhurried prelude, decoratively presented, usually so delicious that one loses interest in what follows. Once, Beirut was celebrated for the best. Two staple ingredients are *hummus* – chick-peas, and *taheena*, sesame oil. The variety of ways in which they can be used is endless, as sauces, or dips, and varied by the spices involved.

But here, a note of caution: if you cannot obtain those particular spices which are the signature of Middle-Eastern food, you must be content to adapt or invent with what is to hand. A few basic spices and herbs which should not be difficult to come by, and should, at any rate, create an Arabian illusion are the following.

Cumin, coriander, saffron, turmeric, black pepper, paprika, pimento (the hot kind called capsicum), ginger, cloves and nutmeg. For herbs, parsley, basil, mint and thyme. A mixture of spices, such as equal quantities of nutmeg, ginger and cloves, ground fine, keep well if tightly corked. Another mixture is made from paprika, black pepper and cloves. Glass jars with cork stoppers are better than tins for storage, and wooden jars (as for fine teas), best of all, for they absorb and retain the heady aroma.

Once upon a happy time, I journeyed about Syria, going from desert to oasis, from Damascus to Ma'loula, a rock village where an ancient language, Aramaic, rather than Arabic, is still spoken and is said to be the language spoken by Jesus. There, climbing dizzily to the fortress-like monastery I ate *falafel*, a rissole made from dried broad beans, the white kind, spiced with garlic and parsley, and deep fried. This is enjoyed throughout the Middle East, from Egypt to Jordan, sometimes dipped in *taheena*, or a mixture of slivered onions steeped in vinegar. On my climb I ate it *nature*. Syrian food remains to me so memorable that sometimes it overcomes any geographic, geo-politic, historic or cultural recollections of my travels.

At Homs, a small, smiling town, the rushing waters of the Orontes river have turned the huge creaking water wheels for centuries, and there are balconied houses and little cafés hanging over streams. There I ate apples stuffed with small pieces of cooked chicken, rice, sultanas, chopped blanched almonds, honey and cloves; which is a good way to make the remains of a chicken go a long way without seeming apologetic. Another Syrian chicken dish is chicken *mish-mishiya* (*mish-mish* being the name for apricots). It is a delicious sweet-and-sour way to vary the ubiquitous fowl. For other things I have eaten among my Arab friends while struggling for as much culinary instruction as I have been able to disentangle, turn to p.168. But if you are going to be lily-livered about experimentation, do not embark on the Arab cuisine. Oddly enough, in all the welter of aromas, garlic is not very much in evidence and none at all is found in salads, where European gastronomes consider a trace or more essential.

Nothing I write on the aromas of Araby would be complete without something about Arab coffee, the fragrant brew which rounds off every repast, welcomes the guest, punctuates the day and is surrounded by as much ceremony as wine-tasting in France. It is in the brewing and serving of coffee that Arab hospitality reaches its apogee. The age-old ritual, with its elegant style of presentation is far more telling than any gargantuan spread. Every palace, house or desert encampment has its coffee hearth and generally a servitor whose sole duty is to prepare the coffee. Such a key post is usually a male prerogative.

The beans are prepared fresh for each brew and must be ground in a stone mortar and roasted over charcoal. The rhythmic sound of pounding, like the seductive smell of the roasting beans is an indivisible part of the Arab scene. Unlike the opaque, rich brew known as Turkish coffee, the Arabic kind is lighter-coloured, almost transparent, and very refreshing. Powdered spices are added, cloves and especially cardamom. Ambergris is a legendary touch of luxury. The guest will always be asked if he wishes his coffee sweet, medium sweet, or unsweetened, and since sugar and coffee are heated together, it is generally simplest to ask for *mazbout* – medium, which should suit everyone. On festive occasions, much sugar is added: in times of sadness, coffee is drunk unsweetened, 'bitter as grief', they tell you, with characteristic poetry.

The cups used are egg-cup-sized china bowls – *finjans* – often painted with a portrait of the local ruler, or with the crescent moon of Islam, and encased in a chased metal or silver holder, the *zarf*. Small as they are, they are only half-filled, for it is considered more elegant to offer very little at a time, burning hot and replenished three times. In the palace or desert camps of the powerful sheiks, the coffee servers are picturesque personages, usually handsome youths. In long robes, sometimes scarlet, belted in gold, they carry round a chased silver and gold beaked coffee pot, and impart a sumptuous air to the ceremony. The flourish with which they serve seems to increase with the status of their master; but one and all have the same curious way of *withdrawing*, rather than approaching the pot to the cup – a drawing back of the arm on high, a kind of legerdemain by which a narrow jet of liquid curves out through the piece of palm frond – *loufa* – used as a filter. It flows direct into the tiny cup, with never a drop spilled. The coffee boy makes the round three times and etiquette demands that on handing back the third cup you will give it a quick, trembling shake. This signifies you will take no more, and will shortly be gone. The third cup is also a polite signal of dismissal. With such refinements does the Arab world, from the Middle East to the furthest Sahara, rich or poor, still embellish daily life.

So much for formalities. As to making Arabic coffee oneself: even having acquired the correct copper, long-handled pot, or *ibrik*, it somehow never turns out quite so delicious, I have found, once away from the charcoal hearth – to say nothing of the dashing coffee-server – and that backward flourish in the act of pouring is not to be attempted under any circumstances.

Tea has come to have its own undisputed place in Arab countries, though with less historic significance, less ritual surrounding it than coffee. Originally, the coffee tree grew wild in Ethiopia and was transplanted to the Yemen, where it flourished and produced the seductive mocha strain. Tea was introduced via the conquering Mongol hordes of Central Asia, who obtained it from China in the form of compressed bricks of dried leaves. This became known as Caravan tea.

The mint tea of Moroccan hospitality is made memorable to me chiefly by the adorable metal tea pots in which it is served: squat, pot-bellied, on little feet, with pagoda-shaped lids, accompanied by big brass and copper kettles, on long-legged stands. Mint tea without these adjuncts seems to me a sticky, over-sugared greenish brew, not green enough to be enticing – more bronzy brown. However it is made decorative by a sprig of mint emerging from the glass in which it is served; even so, its aroma is faintly bitter and cloying too. It lacks those heady wafts that coffee and undreamed of spices combine to produce the true perfumes of Arabia.

CHAPTER 17

My Kind of Christmas Dinner

What is described as the Christmas spirit has become a fierce commercial blackmail which reaches across the world in all its falsity. Holly is flown to Hawaii, there are pink plastic reindeer frosted with *paillettes* in Florida. Hotels in remote lands, where other religions and rites prevail, cash in by charging double for Christmas menus which are local versions of traditional Christian yuletide fare, complete with paper caps and crackers, so that those who have journeyed far afield to escape find themselves trapped once more. Ah! St Nicolas! what crimes are committed in thy name.

Call me Mrs Scrooge, for I propose to retreat into a limbo-land of fantasy, where Darling Self will dream up the only sort of Christmas party Darling Self would really enjoy, and to hell with all the rest. Thanks to the abracadabras and magics of my imaginings, I shall be able to summon all kinds and conditions of guests – twelve people whom I should most like to see gathered round my table, irrespective of centuries or geography, people of today or yesterday, of long ago, or faraway. . . . By some extra-terrestrial magic we shall be endowed with a common tongue, so there will be no bother over communicating. And of course, everyone will be in their prime – that is, the moment of their lives when they are looking and feeling their best, which should make the party go with a swing. Therefore Richard Burton, that darkling adventurer, will have lately returned from his pilgrimage to Mecca. La Dame aux Camélias will have just been launched on *la vie galante* by the Duc de Guiche, and the young Pushkin acclaimed as Russia's greatest poet. . . . But you get the idea.

Before I describe the menu and the setting I have chosen for this singular festivity let me introduce my guests, and round out my list of five women and seven men. Marie Duplessis, the greatest courtesan of Romantic Paris, whom Liszt described as the most perfect incarnation of woman he had ever encountered – and he had encountered quite a few. Such a charmer, of such a profession, will put the men on their mettle – the other women too. Even those of my guests such as St Francis of Assisi or General de Gaulle (for so the President remains to me, forever, remembering his warrior greatness) will, I think, accept her unquestioningly, the General having far too profound a knowledge of human nature, and the past, not to be intrigued by so celebrated a fellow countrywoman. As to St Francis, he had known something of twelfth-century Tuscan revelry in his beginnings: besides, with his limitless charity, he would be the last to condemn; and sinners, redeemable or otherwise, are seldom judged harshly by such as he.

Now for a woman everyone will like on sight, for her classic beauty, charming personality, learning and wide humanity – Lucie, Lady Duff Gordon, who is forever associated with Upper Egypt, where in Luxor in the middle of the last century she came seeking health, and lived and was loved and revered among the people, dying at last among them, far from her family and the brilliant life she had known in London. Her conversation will be as entrancing as her *Letters from Egypt*.

If you look at my seating plan (Plate 8), you will see that except for placing the Mogul Emperor Babur on my right, and King Charles II on my left, I have ignored the delicate question of protocol, putting everyone where I think they will be most harmoniously placed. Thus, beside Lucie Duff Gordon, I am putting the Sultan Qabous bin Saïd, ruler of the Sultanate of Oman, a key figure of Middle Eastern power politics today and extremely handsome too. Besides, his large views on Eastern ladies remaining behind the veil or not, as they choose, seem to me entirely sound (though the ladies little know the stresses that await them with total emancipation). In any case, the sultan can thrash that out with Lady Duff Gordon, who, knowing so well his world, and Koranic principles, might perhaps offer acceptable advice on the thorny questions of modernisation.

Now comes Pushkin, immortal poet, and irresistible to all women, whose talk is as magical as his verse. Garbo shall be next to him – a pleasure for both. Of course Garbo must be present, monosyllabic or no, for she represents immortal beauty. Those bones, those eyelashes are already part of legend. I should have liked to invite Nureyev, another legend, but fear he might accept, and then not turn up, which would be disappointing. On Garbo's right, I put King Charles (and his spaniels, like everybody else's pets will be welcome at my table). Could any hostess ask for a more perfect guest than this saturnine-faced royal charmer, witty, cultivated, generous and kind? And O! how I long to be charmed. ...

I had rather a struggle to decide which of my three central Asian heros I would invite – Tamerlane, 'Timur the Tartar' hero of my childhood's reading, the Mogul Emperor Babur, whose memoirs are my *livre de chevet*, or that wall-eyed old rascal the Maharaja Ranjit Singh, whose extravagant Sikh court and encampments are so vividly described in Fanny and Emily Eden's letters home. Babur won, for we share a deep love of Afghanistan, where he chose to be buried on a hillside overlooking Kabul. (I must not forget to tell him how well his tomb has been restored.) Now comes Queen Marie of Romania, the most romantic of royal figures, who proved a far-seeing politician too. General de Gaulle may enjoy talking Balkan intrigues with her. Then too, her beauty and gaiety will be set off by those fabulous jewels she inherited from her mother (the Tsar Alexander II's only daughter), which she wears with such *panache* – huge *kakoshniks* of diamonds, skipping ropes of pearls, sapphires, rubies. ... No need for a Christmas tree when the candles spark across such glitter.

For obvious reasons, I put Burton and the Sultan of Oman together; the desert will be their meeting point. But if Burton turns to La Dame aux Camélias he may learn something more of Western erotica – he is already master of the Eastern kind. I'm quite sure she will get on well with Pushkin, but then she knew how to get on with most men – as he did with most women.

I've drawn up my seating plan (Plate 8). Or would you care to offer a variation? A page has been left for you overleaf.

I've asked everyone for eight o'clock with magic carpets at midnight. Now let me tell you something about the setting I've chosen. We shall dine on the deck of a *dahabiyeh* (one of those old-fashioned Nile house-boats) moored below the temple of Karnak so that we can watch the moon rise over the Theban hills while the stars rain down round us, reflected in the water as if caught in some gently swaying net. I shan't have any worry about the service, for there will be the traditional Nubian staff, perfect in every respect as they pad round in their graceful long *galabiyehs*, softly attentive, and not yet infected

by the idea that domestic service is lowering. I shall have arrived a bit early to do the flowers (English cottage garden kind, roses and pinks) and to enjoy the whole long, slow magic of sunset with the legendary afterglow – that's a Christmas present in itself.

Which reminds me – did I list the presents my kind guests are bringing me? All the things Darling Self craved. From Pushkin, an ikon for my collection; from St Francis, a rookery, and an elm tree to harbour it; from Lucie Duff Gordon, her perfect knowledge of the Arabic tongue; from Charles II, my likeness by Lely, his court portrait painter; from Queen Marie, a band of her Romanian gypsy musicians – Lautari, for choice; from Burton, those strange secret diaries his wife burned; from the Omani Sultan, a black Bedouin tent; from Garbo, eyelashes as long and as real as her own; from General de Gaulle, a vineyard near Bordeaux; from La Dame aux Camélias, her way with men. . . . Such gifts need no gift wrappings. . . . O! thank you! thank you! . . .

You may well ask what I am giving them? I am giving them the opportunity to skip the centuries and meet people they would not otherwise be able to do.

Do I hear a clatter on the bank? My guests are arriving, punctual to the minute. Here they come! Babur on his elephant, under a gold umbrella; King Charles in a state coach, his spaniels yapping round; a roar overhead, and de Gaulle's helicopter plummets to earth, while Marie Duplessis's elegant little blue coupé spanks up in style. Queen Marie (in full regalia) is managing to look the superb horsewoman she is, dismounting from a plunging stallion without disarranging a jewel. Richard Burton and the Sultan of Oman have both arrived at the same moment, on camels. Out of the cloud of dust they've raised I see St Francis, on foot, surrounded by a flock of birds. Here comes Pushkin, dashing up in a troika (there is still snow powdering the horses' manes). Lucie Duff Gordon has come alongside in her own felucca: she is no stranger to these parts. . . . Now, are we all here? All but Garbo, who telephones she's lost her way, and must be fetched. . . . Or wants to be alone perhaps?

I shall start us off with champagne, of course, while Willie (the King) Smith and his piano, direct from New Orleans, gets things going.

My menu is unconventional for Christmas, save for the pudding, and as I'm no expert on vintages, any really good wines will do, without further fussing.

From Wilder Shores

MENU

25th December, any year

Unlimited caviar
(champagne)

Roast saddle of lamb
Persian rice with raisins
Romaine lettuce salad throbbing with garlic
(Nuits St Georges)

Three perfect cheeses:
Stilton
Greek goat cheese
Pont l'évèque
(Châteauneuf du Pape)

Pause, for a lemon sorbet
then:

English Christmas Pudding
with brandy butter sauce
(Sauterne)

Coffee and liqueurs

Green tea, throughout the meal,
for those who do not touch alcohol

During dinner I shall have Romanian Gypsy music, and with the
sorbet I shall follow the old Persian custom of handing round a
basket full of kittens, playthings, to dandle and fondle, a sort of
furry bouquet, removed, and returned to their mother when the
next course is served. Just before the ritual appearance of the flaming
plum pudding, I have a surprise for everyone. Tolstoy will appear,
dressed in red hood and cotton wool ermine – Father Christmas,
no less, and unloading his sack he will give each of us a snippet of
his great, universal wisdom. With the coffee we shall have another
treat: the voluptuous dancers of Shemakha will sidle in, straight

from the Caucasus, all stiff brocaded finery and clinking ornaments, posturing their age-old pantomimes of desire – but stylishly, no night-club antics here, just a piquant counterpoint to the innocent kittens. I shall wind up with the Russian Tziganes, fetched from one of their legendary St Petersburg haunts. And as we fall silent, overcome by the wild nostalgias they breed, the moon will be seen to sink behind the Valley of the Kings, and lo! the magic carpets unroll along the shore.

Part Two

RECIPES

Breakfast is Best

Oatmeal Porridge

In the Scottish manner since it is a Scottish dish. For four people, 4 breakfast cups of water, a small handful of oatmeal and a pinch of salt; sugar, cream, or milk to taste

When the water reaches boiling point, rain the oatmeal into it with one hand, while stirring continuously with the other. Let it cool for ten minutes, then add the salt, and gently re-heat for another ten minutes. It must not 'catch'. Serve in small bowls, to which each person adds cream or milk (cold). Sugar is heresy, salt is a must.

Kedgeree (the adaptation of an Indian dish, khichri)

1lb smoked haddock, 6oz rice, $\frac{1}{2}$ pint milk, $\frac{1}{2}$ pint water, 4 hard boiled eggs, 2 tablespoons butter, a handful of chopped parsley, salt and pepper, and cream (optional)
(Some people flavour with curry, but I am against this: it over-whelms the haddock.)

Poach fish in milk and water; when done, around 15 minutes, flake gently, removing all skin and bone and any tough bits. Cook rice in water fish was poached in, adding more hot water to amount required to cook rice. Drain rice. Then flake fish lightly into it, add chopped eggs, parsley, butter and seasoning. Place the lot in a well-buttered double boiler, re-heat gently, and stir gently during the process. On no account allow the kedgeree to become a mash.

Devilled Kidneys

Lamb kidneys, grilled with a mixture of Dijon mustard, chili powder and cayenne. A very virile dish, to be served on hot buttered toast.

For two:
Split open 6 kidneys, lengthwise, carefully removing the fatty white core. Thread them between two skewers to keep flat. Make a mixture of fresh butter – about 4 dessertspoons, with 2 of mustard, a pinch of chilli, ditto of cayenne. A dash of lemon juice or wine vinegar is optional. Spread the mixture over the kidneys on both sides before grilling them (moderate heat) for about three minutes each side; but you must judge whether they need a little longer.

Oat Cakes

Perhaps it is my Scottish blood, but no breakfast seems complete to me without oat cakes or bannocks, as they are called, north of the Tweed. They are at once everyday fare and a never-failing treat. Also, they cast a glow of virtue round the eater, for they are extremely healthy food, *and* the slimmers' stand-by.

To make these miraculous biscuits, take half a pound of oatmeal, a pinch of bicarbonate of soda, another of salt, and a dessertspoonful of melted bacon fat. Stir together the oatmeal and bicarbonate of soda, mix well, add salt, make a well in the middle and pour in the melted bacon fat. Knead all together; add a dash of hot water if the mixture is too stiff, or dry. Lay on a board, floured by the oatmeal, and roll out to form a large flat cake, about $\frac{1}{4}$ inch thick. Place on a metal oven sheet and bake for around 15 minutes, then cut into wedge-shaped pieces or rounds. They keep well in a tin (with a lump of sugar, to absorb humidity), but I have never known them remain stored for long; a new batch is always in the making. Delicious with marmalade or honey, or just butter. The young like them with peanut butter.

Afghanistan Remembered

Pushtu Kebab

For four: 4 cups cubed lamb or mutton, fat *and* lean (walnut-sized cubes), enough natural yoghourt (to which a $\frac{1}{4}$ cup of vinegar is added) to cover the pieces of meat, 4 or 5 cloves of garlic cut in slivers, salt and pepper to taste

Leave meat to marinate in this mixture overnight. Turn once or twice. Leave marinating till ready to place in a pan of water with a dash of vinegar added.

Poach the pieces gently for about 3 minutes. Remove, pat dry. Thread on long skewers and grill fast, 3 or 4 minutes. Do not cut off the fat. *Pushtu kebab* is best when fat and lean go side by side, grilled golden.

Some people place chunks of tomato between the pieces. But I do not. Their juice spoils the particular juiciness of *pushtu kebab*, which comes from its yoghourt marinade.

Seshtaranga (a startling dish)

For four: 10 medium-sized onions, $\frac{1}{2}$ breakfast cup of wine vinegar, $\frac{1}{2}$ breakfast cup of brown sugar, 8 eggs, 2 tablespoons vegetable oil, *not* olive – the best is grapeseed oil, salt and pepper

Peel the onions, cut in small chunks, or slice rather thick. Cook in oil till soft, but not brown. Add the vinegar, and simmer till mushy. If they begin to dry up, add a dash of vinegar and water, to keep the onions simmering. When sufficiently soft and almost puréed, add sugar, salt and pepper. Stir thoroughly. While simmering, break the eggs carefully onto the onion purée. As soon as they are set, the *seshtaranga* is done.

Transfer carefully to serving dish, each egg cushioned on onion purée, and serve with crisp brown toast in lieu of *nan* – the wholemeal Afghan bread which is made in long oval pieces, like some speckled leaf.

Pilau Zamrod (Emerald Pilau)

For four: 3 breakfast cups long rice, 2lbs spinach, 3 tablespoons grapeseed or vegetable oil, heaped teaspoon powdered nutmeg

Rinse, coarsely chop the spinach, and cook it in fast boiling salted water till tender – about 10 minutes. Sieve and set aside. Meanwhile, turn rice in mixture of vegetable oil and butter till transparent, but not browned.

Re-heat the spinach water to boiling point, and pour over the rice. Leave to cook uncovered, till 'al dente' – not sloppy. Strain (if any water remains). The rice should have become a very pretty pale green; (more turquoise than emerald, maybe, but green enough).

Re-heat with dabs of butter, and powder with grated nutmeg. *Zamrod* can be eaten with cheese, or meat. I prefer it on its own.

Aft Mewa (The Seven Fruits)

The best kind has mulberries and pistachio nuts ground together with other dried fruits. As a *version* of this Afghan dessert, I suggest a mixture of any available dried fruits worked into a firm purée-like mass.

A cup each of sultanas, dried apricots, peaches, prunes, pears, plums (Elvas are the best), a cup of roughly ground walnuts, or of pistachios, 3 tablespoons honey, with 1 tablespoon lemon juice

Put all together to soak in boiling hot sugared water. Enough *just* to cover the mixture. Leave for 3 or 4 hours at least till very soft. The liquid should have disappeared, leaving a rich gooey mass, hardly able to be stirred. (This is *not* a compote.) Re-heat gently and serve with sour cream.

In Praise of Puddings

Bread and Butter Pudding

A most delicious affair, good for the nursery or the most sophisticated gathering; best eaten hot by the tots, but ice cold, with
lashings of cream (and rum) for the sophisticates. The way of making
it remains the same.

Beat up a bare pint of milk with four eggs and a tea cup of sugar.
Butter, on both sides, eight slices of crustless white bread. Now
butter a pie dish and cover the bottom with overlapping slices of
bread. Sprinkle lavishly with currants and sugar and a dusting of
cinnamon. Repeat the layers till the pie dish is filled. Leave the last
layer, like a lid, but no currants or sugar added. Now make a milk
and egg custard, in the classic manner, adding cinnamon and a
little sugar. Pour this over the bread pudding, slowly, spoonful by
spoonful, giving it time to soak through. Place in a medium oven
for about half an hour, or till the top is a crisp golden crust. Some
cooks dab butter and sugar on it for a final moment under the grill
before serving with cream, or cream, rum and sugar beaten together
as a sauce.

Gooseberry Fool

Or almost any other fruit except melon, apple or pear which would
be insipid. Rhubarb is particularly good. Here are the basic rules:
make a rather firm compote, that is, with very little water. Sieve the
fruit, or put through the mixer, and add almost as much single
cream. Some people mix equal quantities of custard and cream, but
as I have a horror of custard, I don't. Sugar, of course: for gooseberries use white (although I disapprove theoretically of that sort
of refinement), but back to brown for rhubarb.

Suet Pudding

It would be unseemly, after my earlier rhapsodies if I did not give at least one recipe for the machinations that go to making a suet pudding. Moreover I doubt many people take time to make one today: it is a long job and it is *not* recommended for slimmers. But that is no matter here. Now a recipe for one of the several variations: whatever the variation, the basic technique remains the same.

Here it is: to half a pound of flour add two tablespoons of baking powder, two dessertspoons of sugar, a pinch of salt and one and a half cups of finely shredded suet. Mix and add just enough tepid water – a breakfast cup should be enough – to make a stiff dough. This is arduous unless the suet is really properly shredded. Roll out the dough on a floured board to a rectangular shape, about 10 by 16 inches. Spread with a generous layer of golden syrup, or currants and raisins or jam, according to your desire for, respectively, Treacle Pudding, Spotted Dick or Jam Roly Poly.

Now comes the tricky bit. Roll up the dough loosely and put it on a large well-floured tea cloth which has been wrung out in boiling water. Wrap the roll up in this, loosely again, to allow for swelling. Tie each end with string, parcel-like, leaving the two ends of the cloth to be knotted together over the top of the roll like a basket handle (in the making of steak and kidney pudding this same system is used to lift the pudding basin in and out of the boiling water). Now lower your pud into a deep pan of boiling water and let it boil there for about two hours, uncovered. Add more boiling water from time to time, or your pud will be left high and dry and ruined.

To serve, lift out by the knotted handle, untie and place on a 'lordly dish', it deserves no less. 'Send it to table', as old cookery books say, with a sauce of more golden syrup, or jam, according to the nature of the pudding. But Spotted Dick should be sprinkled with brown sugar only. Do not insult its majesty by adding sloppy custards or creams.

Summer Pudding

Red or black currants are the classic fruit for this most sumptuous dish, though raspberries or even blackberries can be substituted. In which case, they are not cooked. The currants must be stewed, as for a compote. Butter medium-thick slices of crustless white bread, and line a deep pudding basin with them, butter side out. The slices should overlap slightly, and cover the bottom too. Now pour in a third of the cooled compote; add a layer of *un-buttered* bread, then more compote, and so on, till the basin is full, and the last layer of bread serves as a lid. Pack down firmly, put a plate on top, and a weight on that. (I use an old iron.) Leave overnight in the refrigerator and turn out with extreme care, so that it does not collapse. The compote will have been completely absorbed by the bread, the whole becoming a delicious, rather soggy mass of a lovely deep crimson colour. Cream, of course, to accompany this treat.

A Syllabub

Whip up double cream, say one tumbler full, and beat in 3 tablespoons of marsala, add $1\frac{1}{2}$ tablespoons caster sugar, 2 beaten egg whites and a little finely grated orange peel. Beat all together furiously, and serve in small glasses, ice cold.

Flummery

This is much in the mood of a syllabub, only more so and of a positively baroque richness, beside the lighter rococo of the syllabub. To half a pint of milk add the same amount of cream(!). Beat together with the yolks of nine eggs, sugar and nutmeg to taste. Heat in a bain-marie 'careful and slow' as the old recipe puts it. Do not stir, but allow it to thicken gradually. When really gooey add a dash of rose water, serve *hot* in little cups. Only very plain biscuits could accompany this. Thin oat cakes perhaps?

Meals on Wheels

Certain dishes served on the original Orient Express were named after some illustrious passenger. I pressed an old Russian friend, once a frequent traveller on the train, for some examples. This extremely vigorous nonagenarian, who attributes his longevity to an indefatigable appetite, rose to the challenge, and recalled, in detail, *filet de sole Carmen Sylva*. Although his gastronomic knowledge and culinary know-how are immense, I fancy he recalled this particular dish chiefly on account of the romantic figure of the poetess – Queen of Romania. She was an ethereal vision, always draped in white veils (one cannot imagine her on the train, let alone eating). Carmen Sylva is not to be confused with her successor, Queen Marie, also much draped, the archetypal Balkan Queen, the embodiment of barbaric splendour, and also difficult to imagine on a train. But back to the *filet de sole* as once served on the Orient Express, and reconstructed for me by my old greedy. Here are his words:

Sole Carmen Sylva

'You are peeling cucumber in small bits. You are poaching it in *vin blanc* and with big big cup of smashed tomatoes and some cayenne – nice and hot. You are putting all through fine *chine* (sieve). Now is becoming beautiful pink juice. You are poaching fish in this but keeping cup of juice to mix with nice roux (butter and flour in the classic manner). Then you are making it more delicious' (eyes now rolling ecstatically) 'with cream and yellow of egg. You are putting such sauce all over the fish then shaking more cayenne over everything before being ready. Mmm...?'

Schalète

When I pressed the old greedy for further recollections of Orient Express specialities, some pudding more interesting than the inevitable pêche melba, he recalled *schalète*, which, it seemed, had once been made at the request of a distinguished figure in the world of high finance, and who had invited my friend to share it with him. *Schalète* is a traditional Jewish dish, though, as my friend reminded me, much like Russian Easter Paskha. Beyond saying it was very sweet, and they had washed it down with champagne and tears (tears of nostalgia?) my old friend seemed unable to supply any helpful details.

No doubt the financier, suddenly overcome with nostalgia, had tipped the chef lavishly, and described the sort of goings-on in the family kitchen of his childhood, so long ago, in some central European ghetto. This is the recipe as given in a book of traditional Jewish cooking:

100 grammes of white bread softened in hot water, drained and mixed with double the quantity of caster sugar. A pound and a half of tart green apples, peeled and sliced, two cups of sultanas, first soaked in rum, added to four well beaten eggs, and mixed together. A buttered soufflé dish is well powdered with sugar, to form a sugary lining, before the fruit mixture is piled in. The *schalète* must be placed in a very hot oven, to 'seize', for a few minutes, and then left in a low oven, to cook slowly for a couple of hours. When cooled, it is turned out, to resemble a sugar-frosted cake.

Pilmeny (a Siberian dumpling)

This is a suety cousin to meat patties found all over central Asia, only *steamed* rather than being the rough, short pastry of the others. In each case the stuffing is much the same, chopped meat and vegetables, recalling Cornish pasties. Among the people of Afghan-Turkestan, in the central Asian steppe country north-east of the Iranian border, this doughy dumpling is called *manti* and is a staple dish, while in Siberia, prepared in exactly the same way, it is called *pilmeny*, batches being made and stored throughout the winter, hung outside, and frozen solid till thawed for use.

Sometimes I make *manti/pilmeny* and munch lovingly, recalling both the Afghan wastes, and my journey across Siberia. It is very easy to prepare, and splendid for using up left-overs, another mark in its favour.

Make a dough of 3 cups of flour to $1\frac{1}{2}$ cups of tepid water. When well kneaded roll out, on a floured board, making a square about $\frac{1}{4}$ inch thick. Cut into little rounds, using perhaps a white wine glass for size. While the dough rests, make the filling of minced, cooked lamb, an equal amount of chopped onion (first lightly fried), chopped mint or dill, and enough butter to make the mixture richly sticky. Drop a heaped teaspoonful on each circle of dough, then fold up and pinch tight at the top, or even tie round, to make a little bundle or pouch. *Pilmeny* should be steamed by whichever method appeals to you: in a perforated metal basket that fits over a saucepan, or one of the Chinese contraptions. If you keep a supply of *ghee* going, use that for sauce, with more mint or dill. In Turkestan the sauce was a rather rank goat cheese, thinned down.

Pozol

This is a rather bucolic brew, a delicious opaque affair which should not be tried out haphazardly. I first tasted it in the tropic heat of southern Mexico, and it has met with approval among my friends during the almost equally flaming heat of August in the south of France.

It is difficult to say to which moment of the day *pozol* is best suited. (Children dote on it at any hour.) In Tehuantepec it was drunk for breakfast, but I doubt that would be right elsewhere. Elevenses possibly or perhaps as a night-cap?

It is simplicity itself – fine-ground corn meal and brown sugar are dissolved slowly in warm water, and whisked up thoroughly (best in an electric beater), then allowed to become ice-cold in the refrigerator. (Never add ice cubes.) Its consistency should be about that of a *very* thin soup, and it can be flavoured faintly with cinnamon. The Mexicans sprinkle it with some mysterious seed, *memay* they said, but I remained baffled.

Kasha Pilaff

I seem to remember that the partisans who held up the Orient Express made a fire of brushwood and cooked some rabbity stew; but I am rather vague about that. A large tin plate of *kasha* and mushrooms was, at one moment, being circulated round; did I eat it? I only remember the mugs of *slivovitz*. Years later I tried the *kasha* mixture in my own kitchen, but added onions.

Since *kasha* (buckwheat groats) is now found in every health shop with directions for its preparation on every packet, I will skip that, only adding that *kasha* is nicer if an egg is forked into it before cooking begins. As every reader knows how to cook onions and mushrooms, I can skip that, too, and simply say that when the *kasha* is cooked, stir in butter generously over high heat before adding the cooked mushrooms and onions. Toss all together, and serve with yoghourt, of course.

Village Inventions
My Roquebrune Kitchen

Ida's Bitter Orange Apéritif

To one bottle of red or white wine (good), add the thin shredded rind of three bitter oranges, about half a pound of sugar, a large wine glass of alcohol* and some camomile flowers. Leave for thirty days, but shake once a day, violently. Sieve, before rebottling. That's all.

Another apéritif I drink in summer is *kir*, thought up by the Abbé Felix Kir at Dijon, far from my region. To one glass of medium dry white wine (and here, it is better if it is an Aligoté de Bourgogne), add one teaspoon of *crème de cassis* (blackcurrant liqueur). But this must be the real thing, no soft-drink syrup will do, for the sweetness *must* be firmly controlled. *Kir* can also be made with *crème de fraises* and champagne.

Aïgou Bolido (Garlic Broth)

Bring a pint or more of salted water to the boil, in which you have put as many peeled cloves of garlic as you like (when cooked, their violence is abated) and a small bunch of sage (if it is stale, or rather dried up, this is of no consequence). Let it simmer. Five minutes before you serve it, throw in a handful of that very fine pasta called *capelli d'angelo* – Angel's Hair; you can also add the yolk of an egg, beaten in quickly when you take the broth off the fire. Two yolks, if you make a big bowlful. Some cheaters add a cube of chicken consommé, on which I frown, in principle, but sometimes use.

*When pure alcohol is unobtainable you might substitute vodka.

Lastly, one dessertspoon of the best olive oil, and, or, a good sprinkle of grated Gruyère.

Rouille

$\frac{1}{2}$ cup white breadcrumbs soaked in milk and drained, 1 egg yolk, 4 cloves of garlic, a coffee spoon of cayenne, paprika and coriander, a pinch of saffron, salt and pepper

Mash or pulp all together and then add $\frac{1}{2}$ cup of warm olive oil, drop by drop as for mayonnaise. This sauce should have the consistency of a custard, if used adventurously to accompany pasta: but if used classically, for fish, it should be much thicker, like whipped cream.

Tunny Fish (my fashion)

4 thick slices of fresh tunny fish. Make incisions all over each, and spike with slivers of garlic. Then brush each slice with olive oil, followed by a lavish spread of tomato purée and a few drops of lemon juice on each slice. Place in a well oiled casserole, cover with foil, and cook in medium oven for about 30 minutes. Baste once or twice, since tunny fish is apt to become dry. At half-time, surround the fish with bananas – not too ripe, and cut lengthwise, and again in half. Sprinkle with a squeeze of lemon, salt and pepper. They will not take long to cook.

Brandade of Salted Cod

Soak the salted fish for a whole day and rinse well. Bring to the boil in fresh water and remove bones. Flake the flesh, together with 4 or 5 crushed cloves of garlic. Let it simmer for a short while: see that it is very soft and smooth. Heat a small saucepan of milk and another of olive oil until well warmed, but not boiling. All the ingredients should be kept at about the same temperature. Then, bit by bit (a laborious process), add, driblet by driblet, warm milk, warm oil, milk, oil and so on, stirring all the while till a homogeneous mass is achieved. Some people in the Midi add chips of black olives and parsley. Always serve with triangles of fried bread, whether you are eating it hot or cold. I prefer it hot.

My loved and lamented Monte Carlo neighbour, Douglas Cooper, art historian and arch-gourmet, used to add truffles, which I thought rather too much of a good thing – too much in the taste of Mammonville, as I now called Monte Carlo.

Artichokes à la Barigoule

Cut off the stalks of artichokes. Cut the leaves down to half so that they open a little. Extract the stringy, straw-like centre, and fill with chopped, cooked mushrooms and carrots, plenty of garlic, cooked rice, parsley, and the delicate *fond d'artichaut*. Sprinkle well with lemon juice and a teaspoon of olive oil in each artichoke. Place them, tightly packed together, in an open cocotte; they must be well packed, or they risk spreading – even collapsing. (I sometimes tie mine up with string.) Add a wine glass of wine, one tumbler of bouillon (chicken cube will do), and one wine glass of olive oil, and if you like some tomato purée. Leave the artichokes to simmer in this sauce for a good hour, on very low heat or in a low oven. The cocotte must be covered tightly.

Tourte

This can be made with marrow, chard leaves, or, best of all, artichoke hearts. Blanch in boiling water for 5 to 10 minutes, then squeeze as dry as possible. Meanwhile, make a short pastry, with water and oil, well salted. Form a round tart. Keep aside enough for lid. To fill: grate unpeeled marrow, cut the chard coarsely, sauté onions, add shredded marrow or artichokes. Add some rice just barely cooked in salted water (8 minutes). Mix all together with beaten egg. Spread on pastry casing. Dust with salt and pepper and chopped parsley. Add pastry lid. Pinch edges well and place on an oiled platter in medium oven for $\frac{1}{2}$ hour or more, according to your pastry – or your oven, come to that.

Babajuin (Ida's way)

Make a thin short pastry. Roll out flat, to about twenty-four inches long and six to eight inches wide. This will give you twelve *babajuins*, or little turnover pastries. On the long strip of pastry dough, place at the extreme left, a dollop of the filling (cooked rice, chopped cooked onion, grated Gruyère cheese and if possible some scraps of ham and an egg). Fold over the pastry to form a well-sealed pasty;

give the dough a twist to separate the first pasty from the next and so on all down the line. Then either separate each one or cut the long roll in half, and fry in scalding oil for a few moments. Serve hot or cold, with a tomato sauce if you like.

Lemon Curd (Lemon Preserve, made from our village lemons)

$\frac{1}{4}$ pound of butter, 1 pound lump sugar, grated rind of two lemons and juice of three lemons. Stir the mixture till sugar is all dissolved. Add six beaten eggs, yolks and whites. Stir till the mixture starts to thicken over a *very low* flame. It must *not* boil. When ready, it is like a thick honey. Store in jam jars, well sealed. Or just buy it ready made.

Lost Lemon Pudding

This rather resembles the classic English Summer Pudding, in that you use thin slices of white bread (crust removed, of course), spread lavishly with the lemon curd. Line a buttered glass bowl with the slices. In the centre of the bowl, place a little jar which fills the centre space. Pack round it with smaller slices of the lemon-spread bread till the pudding basin is full. Pour the juice of two fresh lemons over everything, and sprinkle thickly with grated lemon rind. Leave overnight in the refrigerator. To serve, remove the jar, fill the centre with whipped cream or a lemon sorbet, or lemon ice-cream, to be party-ish. You can also decorate this delight with a ring of very thin lemon slices, just to hammer home the point.

Bread and Velvet
Turkish Delights

Yogurtlu Çorba (or Turquoise Soup, as it was poetically described to me)

This is a variation of the many yoghourt-based soups found in Turkey, and all over the Middle East. If the soup is to be a cold one, uncooked, the pale greenish tint is arrived at by stirring in some finely-shredded cooked spinach or watercress mixed in while hot, and left to cool, in the yoghourt. If a hot soup is desired, the yoghourt must be stabilised, as always, and prevented from curdling in the heat by the addition of flour or egg.

For the cold soup

4 cups of yoghourt, 4 tablespoons of finely shredded spinach or watercress, a cucumber, peeled and sliced thinly, salted to drain, before using, some sprigs of mint, as many chips of garlic as you please, salt and pepper, juice of $\frac{1}{2}$ lemon

Mix all together, and serve in a big bowl, sprinkled with snippets of mint or bright green chives, to strengthen the turquoise illusion.

For the hot soup

Same ingredients, plus: 2 cups of yoghourt, one onion finely sliced, 1 dessertspoon of flour, 2 cups of chicken broth

Begin by frying the onion lightly. Then heat the yoghourt gently, stirring in the flour. Add 2 large cupfuls of chicken broth, or 1 cube dissolved in the same amount of water, and simmer, adding the cucumber slices, *not* peeled, this time, and the uncooked shredded spinach, or watercress, and a pinch of bicarbonate of soda. Simmer all together, with or without slivers of garlic, but plenty of salt and pepper. When a faintly turquoise hue is obtained, remove from the stove and add lemon juice and serve powdered with crushed walnut, and finely snipped watercress or chives sprinkled over the surface.

Börek

I am no hand at pastry: I buy the ready prepared kind, puff, or short, without shame, and suggest you do the same. For *börek* use the flaky kind (called *yufka* in Turkey).

Prepare the pastry as directed on the packet – or go your own way, if you know how. Roll it out till it is as thin as possible – or thinner. Leave in a cool place while you prepare one of the following fillings.

Cream cheese, well salted, with herbs such as cumin, oregano, or estragon

Fine-minced cooked meat, with paprika and pine nuts

Cooked spinach, snipped fine, and bound with a very little thick cream

Now roll out your pastry once again to get it almost transparent before you cut it into four inch squares on which you place a spoonful of the filling. Fold, envelope fashion, or just in half, and twist up the ends slightly. Or roll, cigarette fashion. For this it is better to cut the pastry into rectangles. Brush over with beaten egg and bake as directed on the packet. Usually a hot oven, for about half an hour, is long enough.

Kadin Budu Köftesi (Ladies' Thighs)

This voluptuously named dish is, prosaically, rissoles, no more, no less, but so named because of its particular form, and texture, as plump and soft as any limb an odalisque could offer a pacha.

1lb of lamb, minced fine, or put through a blender with the onions, 2 medium onions shredded very fine, 1 egg, 1 dessertspoon chopped parsley or dill, 2 tablespoons heavy cream (or fresh butter), 4 tablespoons cooked rice, olive or sesame oil, salt and a sprinkle of nutmeg, flour

Lightly fry the mince and onions together. Add the yoke of one egg and the rice and work into a smooth mixture, with the shredded parsley or dill, and flavour to taste. When a really homogeneous mass is achieved, add the cream and mix once again. Then mould into little sausagey shapes. Dust over with flour, and fry. The *köftesi* should be a pale golden colour, not too browned, or they will be dry. A lemon and butter sauce is good with this dish.

Ekmek Serai (Palace Bread)

A loaf of very stale white bread (although I use light brown), 1 cup of clear honey, 1 cup of white sugar, juice of 1 lemon, 1 cup of chopped pistachio nuts, thick, or double cream (optional)

Remove crusts from bread and cut into rather thick slices – perhaps even one inch thick. Prepare a syrup of sugar, honey and lemon juice simmered together with a dash of water if it becomes too solid (classically, orange or rose water should be used), and bring to the boil.

Now put the bread slices in a large shallow baking dish, and pour the syrup over them. There must be enough to cover the bread completely. Leave on a very low flame, or better on a mat to avoid burning. Press the slices gently so that they soak up all the syrup. When this is thoroughly done, remove from the heat, and allow to cool for a few minutes before lifting the slices out (a flat fish server is good for this). Arrange the golden slices on a big dish, and sprinkle with chopped pistachio nuts – and why not go the whole hog and souse them with cream? There must be no nonsense about liver, or line, here.

Ekmek Kâdife (Bread and Velvet)

The simplest yet most audacious and stylish dish. Stylish because of its very simplicity, audacious for it takes a lot of savoir-faire to offer this, at the end of a dinner party. But I have never known it fail to please, once the astonishment is overcome.

A number of small, rather thick fingers of coarse-grained brown bread on the stale side, served in a basket, and a large bowl of the thickest fresh cream

Each person takes a few fingers of bread, and a huge spoonful of cream, which they pile, mouthful by mouthful, on the bread fingers.

That's all: no sugar, no jam (rose petal is best if you wish to cheat). The secret of this dish is the contrasting textures: the grainy bread, and the suave cream, which of course must be freshest of the fresh and as heavy as possible to resemble Kaïmak, the superbly rich Turkish cream from buffalo milk.

Turkish Coffee

To make Turkish coffee, see 'Arabian Aromas,' p.171.

Count Rumford's Soup and Some Others

Count Rumford's Soup

The count's basic recipe, as I found it in a Victorian cookery book of modest nature. The recipe can be varied or given more luxurious additions according to whim. The quantities given, while seeming insufficient for the Bavarian poor, still seem suited to a *very* large household. But I leave it as it stands, for the adapter to adapt.

Simmer slowly 8oz barley, and 6oz shelled peas in 4 quarts water; allow several hours, till all is really tender. Add 2lbs of peeled potatoes, 2oz coarse salt, $\frac{1}{2}$ teaspoon pepper, a large bunch of fresh herbs, and 4oz of wine vinegar. When all is cooked through, stir in 8oz of stale brown bread broken into small pieces. Thin with boiling water if required. Onions, carrots, turnips, and their tops, celery, cabbage, dandelion leaves, and the outside of lettuce leaves, etc. can be added to the basic ingredients to vary the flavour.

Cullen Skink

A fishy version of Skink proper, a Scottish meat and vegetable soupy stew. Finnan haddock is skinned and gently poached in boiling water to cover, with one good-sized onion coarsely chopped. As soon as the haddock is cooked (about 15 to 20 minutes), remove the bones and flake the fish. Return the bones and bits to the oniony water, and simmer for at least half an hour, before straining. A bay leaf adds to the flavour. Meanwhile boil up a pint of milk, and add to the fish stock, before replacing the pieces of fish. Finally, have ready about 2 cups of mashed potato (mashed very smooth with a lot of butter or margarine) and spoon this into the soup bit by bit until you obtain a thick, but not heavy consistency. Add plenty of pepper, but go easy on the salt.

Garlic Broth, or Aïgou Bolido

I have described this health-giving soup on p.130 when evoking the resources of my Mediterranean village kitchen. Garlic has proven powers to reduce high blood pressure, and induce slumber. Now since Tension, like Cholesterol and the ogre Overweight are fashionable preoccupations, garlic's curative powers should silence any finicky criticism of its anti-social nature. A brew of strong black coffee is said to overcome the fumes if taken immediately after an over-indulgence in garlic. . . . On the other hand, it might undermine the calming properties of the garlic. For you to choose.

Cucumber Soup

This is a variation of Balkan yoghourt soup (see p.134), found alike in Yugoslavia, Turkey and Greece, under different names, but with little difference. Essentially, it is a cold, summer soup. This version only has yoghourt added as a trimming at the point of serving, whether the soup is hot or cold.

Cut a large, unpeeled cucumber into chunks, add one or two medium-sized onions, chopped fine, and soften them delicately in butter. Add two pints of water, a medium-sized potato diced, and a large bouquet of watercress. Stew all together very slowly till the vegetables are really soft. Add salt and pepper, a knob of butter, and pass through the mixer to obtain a creamy, greenish coloured soup. Sour cream (or yoghourt) is added at the moment of serving, along with a few slices of peeled fresh cucumber, and a sprinkling of fresh dill. (Powdered must do if fresh is unobtainable.) Dill is one of the few herbs that retain a certain pungency in dried form.

Lettuce Soup

This is a variation of the above, simply substituting finely chopped or shredded lettuce for the cucumber, and instead of dill, using mint. Add half a lemon, in slivers, while the soup simmers. A dash of lemon juice, like fresh cream, is an addition, when serving.

Palestinian Purée

This is an old name for a thick soup made from those delicious knobbly tubers which we call Jerusalem artichokes (perhaps the Crusaders first brought them back from what was then Palestine, the Holy Land). The French call them *topinambour*. During World War II they became a monotonous diet for certain starving regions of occupied France, and in consequence have been unpopular there ever since, like all reminders of unpleasant times. Which is unfair on this vegetable whose subtle flavour is, to me, even worthy of challenging the truffle. I like it as a purée, mixed with potatoes, as itself, with melted butter and parsley, to accompany a roast, but best of all as a very suave soup.

To make Palestinian Purée first steel yourself to the bother – for that it is – of peeling their knobbed surface. The best way is to parboil them rapidly, and then the thin skins scrape off more easily.

1½lbs of peeled artichokes, sliced or in small chunks, should be placed at once (to prevent discoloration) into a saucepan of milk and water (about 1 pint). Allow to stew until tender. Sieve or put through mixer: add a large knob of butter and a little cream, but hardly even a pinch of salt here, as the flavour is so delicate. Beat well together. If the mixture is too thick, add warm milk with caution: this soup should be very thick – almost disinclined to drop off the spoon.

Carrot Broth (my way)

Here is a particularly decorative soup, like one of those rosy, apricot-hued marbles of Italy.

1lb of finely sliced carrots, one large onion or two medium ones, roughly chopped. Turn well in butter, or vegetable oil. When softened, but not browned, add a pint and a half of hot water, salt and pepper, 2 lumps of brown sugar, and pieces of lemon cut into chunks, but not peeled. Simmer all slowly for about an hour. Top up the water, if there is too much evaporation (but a tight-fitting lid should prevent this). The broth can be sieved, and served as a clear soup, with croutons and a sprinkle of chives, or put through the mixer, to become creamy, thick, apricot-coloured and delicious served cold, very cold, with yoghourt swirled lightly round at the moment of serving so that a pretty, marbled pattern is obtained.

Nettle Soup

Select young, green nettle tops, preferably picked away from hedges or ditches where car-fumes threaten. Wash in salted water and chop very fine. Simmer in a light stock – chicken (or a chicken cube will do) – for about an hour. Salt and pepper, a dash of vinegar and a lump of sugar should be added. A small clove of garlic can give zest, and there are two minds as to whether a few spoonfuls of pearl barley or wild rice should be added for body. A large quantity of nettles are needed, since they diminish greatly in the cooking. If you have added the barley or rice, then you will not strain the soup, but serve it all together. If you strain it, you will have a light, translucent broth of great delicacy.

Queen Victoria's Soup

I quote: 'For a dozen persons, take three plump fowls, skinned, and a large bunch of parsley, simmer them in a strong veal broth for $1\frac{1}{2}$ to 2 hours. The flesh must then be removed and pounded with two French rolls previously soaked in the broth. The yolks of 6 hard boiled eggs, and a tablespoon of ground almonds are now added, the whole to be well pounded, as much salt and pepper as judiciously may be added, with a quart of cream previously heated to boiling point.'

Those were the days.

Avocado Summer Soup

Two large, almost over-ripe avocados – those which peel easily are essential. Mash the flesh together with three or four spring onions (no green tops), about 2 dessertspoons of chopped parsley, a carton of natural yoghourt, the juice of one large lemon and a breakfast cup of water. Salt and pepper to taste – but the lemon makes it very sharp.

Beat up again or put through the blender. Add more yoghourt or water according to the consistency required (it should be a *thick* soup), and leave in refrigerator for at least three or four hours – overnight even.

This soup is a close cousin to the more solidified Arabian dish called *baba ganoush*, see p.169. But I prefer these same basic ingredients presented, or thinned out, as a summer soup.

Russian Traditional

Sauerkraut Stchee à la Stravinsky

This is a variation of Russian cabbage soup – if you go for that rather violent creation. I was introduced to it by Madame Vera Stravinsky, when she and the composer were in Hollywood, where she kept a small house to which she sometimes retired to paint her strange, lyrical visions. But she was very down to earth in the kitchen, and gave me the following recipe:

One pound of ready-cooked choucroute (obtainable from a delicatessen store). Press out all the liquid and leave to drain. Shred as small as possible together with two finely shredded onions. Turn the mixture in a *little* bacon fat, 2 or 3 minutes at most. Add a tablespoon of tomato purée, the same of flour, and a dessertspoonful of brown sugar to the onion and sauerkraut mixture. Finally, add 3 cupfuls of clear meat broth or consommé. Stir well, leave to simmer for no more than 5 minutes; then allow to cool slowly, and leave standing in the refrigerator overnight. Re-heat, to serve, adding plenty of sour cream.

Oukha (fish soup from Siberia)

Less a soup, like *bouillabaisse*, than a clear broth, classically made with fresh-water fish, but use any white fish, not skinned or boned: only heads and tails removed. Bring slowly to the boil. Four pints of water for 2lbs of fish, to which onions, celery, parsley and carrots are added. Add plenty of salt and pepper. A red or green pepper, skinned and chopped fine, fiery seeds removed, adds to the flavour. Simmer for 2 hours. Strain and serve sprinkled with fresh chopped dill.

Kalajosh (lamb stew from the Caucasus)

6 dessertspoons of olive oil, 1lb lamb meat, cut into small cubes, 2 large onions chopped fine, plenty of chopped garlic, salt and pepper, 4 thick slices of *white* bread, fresh yoghourt, to which can be added, half and half, some sour cream.

Fry meat and onion till golden; add coriander, garlic and bread, cut in $\frac{1}{2}$ inch cubes, and fry gently till all is crisp, but not dried up. Add more oil if necessary. Salt and pepper to taste. Serve yoghourt in a dish apart, as sauce – to which chopped mint or dill can be added.

Walnut Sauce (Satsivi – a Georgian speciality)

1 cup of walnuts, shelled and pounded, 1 large clove of garlic, 1 small onion chopped fine, salt, pepper, saffron and cayenne pepper added generously, the whole mashed to a thick paste with a little chicken broth and wine vinegar. Consistency should be on the thick side. Can be served with fish, meat, or vegetables.

Mushroom Sauce (a Slav standby for fish, meat or vegetables)

$\frac{1}{2}$ lb of mushrooms slightly cooked in melted butter (*not* margarine), then a little milk added, and slowly simmered for 15 minutes: if the milk boils almost away add a little bouillon: sprinkle with flour to thicken, or add a *little* more milk and an egg, and put through the mixer so a thickish purée is obtained. Add salt and pepper and a squeeze of lemon. Excellent with plain boiled potatoes.

Tkemali (plum sauce, another Caucasian delight which transforms left-over cold meat, or game)

Half a cup of plum or damson jam (a good brand, not too sugary), and 2 tablespoons of red wine vinegar. Heat together with a clove of garlic chopped fine, a teaspoon of coriander, another of all-spice, and another of paprika. Salt and pepper as you please. Simmer the mixture, and then sieve it to the consistency of a rather thin purée. If it becomes too runny, add more jam, but be careful that the sharp, vinegary flavour is not lost.

My Lightening Blini

That is, the kind that is almost idiot-proof and requires none of the exactitudes that classic *blini* demand. My version is garbled, I know, for when my old Katusha made the real thing she insisted on a Russian friend coming round to help – to give moral support, it was inferred, since the whole proceeding was in the nature of a sacred ritual. I was never allowed to watch, but I gathered the mixture of sour milk, flour etc. had to be made some hours in advance and left to rest in a darkened corner ... anyhow, the final result was always a perfection of delicacy, with no resemblance to those thick muffiny things which restaurants too often serve as *blini*, today. Nevertheless, here is my idiot kind, without pretension or apology.

To one cup of white flour, sifted, add one tablespoon of baking powder, and mix together. Make a well, and pour in one and a half cups of tepid milk with two tablespoons of sour cream. Beat two eggs frothily and add to the rest, with a teaspoon of salt. Stir all together or put through the mixer. Then set aside for a bare half hour. When the frying pan is smoking hot, with good fresh butter, add little dollops of the *blini* mixture: keep the finished *blini* not more than 5 inches across. Pile them up in a hot napkin and eat with more sour cream or with melted butter or both – and red caviar, or black lumpen-fish, or salted herrings, or smoked trout, which is lighter than smoked salmon. Or, of course, caviar itself, if you can lay your hands on it.

Paskha

A simplified version of this classic Easter dish can be made by beating the yolks of four eggs into two pounds of a firm cottage cheese with ¼lb of sweet butter and a breakfast cup of heavy cream. Add another cupful of caster sugar which has been perfumed (over-night) by a stick of cinnamon. Beat the mixture furiously, or cut time and effort by using an electric blender. Next, add a cup of candied fruit chopped fine, some sultanas (first puffed out by soaking in warm water) and perhaps some glacé cherries, also chopped fine. A dessertspoonful of lemon juice can be added. Mould the whole mass into a rough pyramid (in Russia special blunt-topped, cone-shaped wooden moulds are used.)* Tie it up in a cheese cloth, and hang the bundle over a basin so that the whey drips out. In twelve hours or so, there will be no more drips. Then pile the whole into the classic blunt-topped cone-shape and refrigerate for 24 hours before serving.

*Note: an ordinary flower-pot makes quite a good mould.

The Wilder Shores
of Picnicking

English sausages, like French garlic loaves or Italian pizzas are naturals for picnics. But here are some alternatives. Dips, if interesting ones, make good picnic starters. However, there must be no nonsense about potato chips. Really good crisp breads, biscuits or cheese straws are better. For a dynamic dip try *rouille* (rust, on account of its colour), a Provençal speciality usually served as a sauce with fish, or that majestic fish soup *bouillabaisse*. Here it is in full detail.

Taheena

This is another unexpected dip, hailing from the Lebanon. It derives from sesame-seed oil. Buy it ready prepared, as a thick paste, from Oriental delicatessen stores. Mix with water to thin, mash in a little chopped parsley, a dash of lemon juice and a lot of salt.

Aïoli

This is simply a good stiff mayonnaise with as much pounded garlic as you care to add. Try it with tunny fish sandwiches, or as a variant to horse-radish, with cold beef sandwiches.

Tapénade

Here thin slices of cold chicken or turkey are galvanised out of the usual monotony by being very lightly touched with *tapénade*, the dark, astringent olive, caper and anchovy spread, of Italian derivation.

Bouloni

This Afghan standby was mine when on the road across that wild land. Make a short-crust pastry with wholemeal flour. Roll out to a rectangle and cut this into smaller rectangles, say 8 by 4 inches. Then fill each with a mixture of spring onion tops and or the tenderest green of leek tops (first poached in milk, squeezed dry and well salted and peppered). Brush these narrow packets over with oil or milk – be sure their edges are crimped shut – and bake till well browned.

Cornish Pasties

These are also a perfect picnic food, as transportable as delicious. To make, short-crust pastry is rolled out to nine or ten inch rounds, and then filled with snippets of lean steak, *raw*, like the small potatoes, thinly sliced. Onions and sliced turnips also uncooked, and well seasoned, are placed in layers on half the round of pastry dough. Potato first, then the other vegetables, and lastly, the meat. The unfilled half folds over like a lid, to form a half moon shaped pasty. Scrimp the edges, brush over with butter, and bake in a medium oven for around 40 to 50 minutes.

Eggah

This is a sort of upright-standing cakey omelette much liked in the Middle East.

Twelve eggs beaten up with salt, pepper and plenty of finely chopped parsley. Pour into a heavy-based deep frying pan in which 3 table-spoons of butter are sizzling. Cover and leave on very low heat for 15 to 20 minutes – until the whole thing is set firm and can be cut like a cake, and eaten hot or cold.

Lastly to 'warm the cockles of the heart', I suggest a thermos of *Glühwein* (mulled wine) or strong tea laced with ginger, such as Egyptians enjoy during brief wintry spells.

Recipes

Glühwein

In a saucepan boil up 1 pint of red wine (claret best), 2 slices of lemon, $\frac{1}{4}$ stick of cinnamon, or 2 teaspoonfuls of the powdered kind, 3 or 4 lumps of sugar, and a half a coffee spoon of cloves.

Ginger Tea

Make an infusion of Indian tea, fairly strong. For four cups, add 3 teaspoons of powdered ginger and 4 or more lumps of sugar. This must be drunk scalding hot. You will notice I have in mind the sort of summer weather which, alas!, calls for hot drinks so, look to your thermos.

The Turquoise Table
Traditional Persian Food

Here are some Persian sauces, by which the housewife varies the staple rice pilaff. These sauces are rich and stew-like, and make a very little meat go a long way, and as I have remarked earlier, are the glory of the Persian cuisine.

Khoresh Beh (quince sauce)

Core and slice 4 to 6 quinces, fry in butter and set aside. Fry one pound of beef cut in small chunks, with a large onion in small dice; add a teaspoon of cinnamon, half a teaspoon of nutmeg, two tablespoons of sugar. When all is browned, simmer in the juice of half a lemon and two cups of water. Salt and pepper the mixture rather heavily. Leave on low fire, covered, for at least half an hour. About 10 minutes before serving add the quince slices, stirring gently into the rest. The resulting *khoresh* should be rich and sharp. If it does not have sufficient body, add a little butter rolled in flour to thicken the sauce; some cooks add a few spoonfuls of dried peas, to simmer with the rest.

Khoresh Fesanjan

The same principle applies to numbers of other sauces, such as *khoresh fesanjan* which is chicken pieces with fresh pomegranate juice, finely chopped walnuts and a touch of tomato sauce (ready made will do), simmered together. Onion, salt and pepper, lemon juice and sugar added, as in the *khoresh beh*.

Khoresh Sak

This is a spinach and orange mixture, much enjoyed along the shores of the Caspian, where there are many orange groves. One pound of minced beef is made into small, walnut-sized balls and fried in butter or oil. Two pounds of spinach chopped fine, along with a large onion and some parsley are also fried; then, together with the beef balls, and a clove of garlic, a teaspoon of cinnamon and another of oregano and a dessertspoon of sugar, all is left to simmer in two cups of orange juice and one of lemon juice with a very little water added. Salt and pepper and perhaps a little flour to thicken, at half time.

Ashe Sholeh Gholam Khar
(one of the many ashe, or thick soups)

Stew two pounds of chopped leeks and onions, with two cups of kidney beans, parsley, salt, pepper and tumen: strain and set aside. Now stew a pound of meat, beef or lamb, although beef is best and a cheap cut will do here. When rather over-cooked, mash until pulpy, with two cups of cooked rice. Fry the vegetable mixture you had set aside (walnut oil is particularly good for this), and add to the purée-like meat and rice mixture and moisten with a very little of the vegetable water. Re-heat and serve, in little bowls, with wooden spoons. *Ashe* should be very very thick, as it is in the *bas fonds* of the bazaars in provincial towns where there are small eating-houses or *tchai-khanas* which serve nothing else. I was not popular with my more selective friends when I begged to stop for a bowlful.

Polo

Polo is the Persian pilaff. Everyone has their own fool-proof way to prepare a pilaff, which of course must never, in any way resemble Italian risotto.

Rice for pilaff must be something between dry and fluffy, never hard like failed rice, or soft, like the delicious Italian risotto. Persian cooks used to rather show off about the three kinds of rice obtainable, roughly first, second, and third class, and the various ways of cooking each. The three basic rice dishes are *chelo, polo* or *kateh*. *Chelo* is steamed rice, served with one of the special sauces, or, as in *chelo kebab*, with meat *kebabs* and a raw-egg sauce which I have eulogised on p. 69. *Polo* is rice cooked in water. *How* is a matter of never-ending discussion, outside of the Persian kitchen. The proportions are generally 2 cups of well-washed rice to four cups of water. Cover, and cook over a low heat till all water is absorbed.

To make *kateh*, follow the same directions but when all the water is gone, stir well, and add two tablespoons of butter and one of oil; cover again and leave for half an hour on a very low fire. Then, with a flat fish slice or wooden spatula, work round the edges of the rice, and turn it out, upside down. A lovely crisp golden top (which was at the bottom) should now be discovered and eaten as the *pièce de resistance*. In the Holy City of Meshed they told me that properly cooked *polo* is so light it rises up (miraculously) however hard it's pressed down.

For myself, having observed the ways of many nations with rice, I cook it as simply as possible. I buy the long-grain kind; I don't rinse it, but turn it in fast-cooking oil, till every grain is coated. Then I souse it in boiling water just enough to cover, and cook uncovered, till all the water has gone. I then put a cloth over it and leave it in a fairly hot oven, to absorb the steam, for about five minutes. That's all. It usually works: but rice can be very unpredictable and unnerving.

Sekanjaban Syrup

This can be eaten with lettuce (see p. 70) or diluted with water as a refreshing summer drink.

For the basic syrup, put six cups of white sugar in 2 cups of water, with one cup of vinegar, and some crushed mint. Heat the sugar and when dissolved, add the vinegar and simmer for a quarter of an hour. Chill, but add the mint while it is still warmish. Do not put in the refrigerator.

Bitter cherries, frosted over with icing sugar, were sometimes offered at the end of dinner, and gave a curiously sophisticated air to the customary glass of tea, as they were crowded onto the saucer beside it. They were a welcome change from sickly cakelets or those after-dinner chocolate mints much favoured in the West.

Eating for France
Diplomatic Dinners

I shall not give here recipes for any of the elaborate but banal dishes which I ate with monotonous regularity while *en poste*. They are the tried classics, to be found in every book on *la cuisine française*, and on every diplomatic table too.

But while *en poste*, there were occasionally small impromptu Sunday night suppers which broke the monotony of the usual diplomatic round, for the hostess herself might prepare a typical dish from her native land (or at any rate, generally claimed to have done so). 'The staff are all off tonight, so come just as you are and we'll rustle up something', was the tone of the invitation. Here are a few national dishes I came to regard as Sunday Night Specials.

Guma Plov (an Azerbaijani pilaff as served at a Turkish Embassy)

This pilaff is particularly exotic. Ground lamb is sautéd in butter with fine chopped onions (not cut in rings). Dried currants or sultanas (first soaked in hot water) and stoned cherries (or dried prunes) are added, and turned with the lamb and onions. But chestnuts are the essentials here, peeled, chopped fine and cooked gently in butter before being added to the rest. Serve the mixture on a mound of plain saffron rice. When I ate this same dish in Konyia a sauce of pomegranate juice was also offered.

Mente Küfte (an Albanian dish as served at a Yugoslav Embassy)

This is simply meat balls (the usual routine of minced meat, mixed with breadcrumbs, beaten eggs and flour) with *plenty* of chopped fresh mint added, and if you like it, a sprinkling of cinnamon. The old Russian cook who made these was persuaded to give me his opinion of such exoticism. He thought both the mint and the cinnamon heresy, and stood firmly by the classic Russian *cotletki*, small minced meat balls with bread and onions added, fried in egg, but no more nonsense, as he put it.

Feijao (served at a Brazilian Embassy)

This black bean stew, heavy, perhaps, but how good, is cooked with a purée of tomatoes, onions, and a chunk of fatty salt bacon. The beans are first soaked in cold water overnight and then simmered for some hours; when soft, the other ingredients are added, and the whole thing is again simmered for as long as you please. The longer the better. I add a lump or two of brown sugar, to bring up the flavour.

Kabouni

Another Albanian rice dish served among the Bulgarians from whose cook I obtained the recipe. I have found it a good stand-by for cold meat of a scrappy kind, quite removing it from the cold cuts and pickle stigma.

Kabouni is simply long-grained rice cooked as for a pilaff, in veal or chicken stock, with raisins added, and *lavishly* flavoured with powdered nutmeg and coriander, but of course, salt and pepper too, for this is *not* a pudding. When I make it I add fine-chopped onions lightly browned in butter, and forked into the cooked rice along with the raisins, just before serving.

The rice should be very hot, even though surrounding the cold cuts. Slices of cold lamb alternating with pieces of cold turkey were what the Bulgarians gave us. Outside the rice was another ring of sliced red peppers and dill pickles, the sweet–sour Russian or Jewish kind, with a sour-cream dressing. This was in piquant contrast to the almost flowery fragrance of the spiced rice, yet somehow, it went well together.

Pudim Portuguez (from a Portuguese Consulate)

This celebrated pudding recalls an Italian *zabaglione* but has no Marsala or any wine added to its sumptuosity.

A whole pound of sugar (white) is heated together with the juice of 5 large oranges and the grated zest of one. As it begins to thicken, but before it caramelises, it is removed from the fire, and allowed to cool. When almost cold, the yolks of ten eggs, first well beaten, are stirred in. The mixture is poured into a buttered soufflé dish (or any fire-proof one) which is rubbed round with butter. This is then placed in a bain-marie and simmered till it sets firm. When quite cold, it is eased out of the soufflé dish, sprinkled with more grated orange peel and left for some hours in the refrigerator. We ate this delicacy from little blue and white dishes (Portuguese ware) which recalled the blueness and whiteness of the lovely Azuelos tiles which adorn the walls of churches, palaces and gardens everywhere in that enchanting land.

Ma'Mounia (from an Egyptian Embassy)

Ma'Mounia is a delectable pudding, famous all over the Middle East and North Africa too; but it has nothing to do with Morocco's celebrated hotel, the Mamounia, at Marrakesh. Both hotel and pudding take their name from the Caliph Ma'Moun, who was Hārūn al-Rashid's son. The pudding is pure Arabian Nights, and very easy to make. These were the directions given me by the Syrian cook (Syrians consider it one of their specialities).

Make a syrup with one pint of water, the juice of half a lemon and a cup of sugar (white). Simmer for ten minutes or so, and set aside. Then melt a teacup of butter, and when sizzling add a rather larger cup of semolina, and fry, stirring all the while, for about 5 minutes. Then add the syrup, and beat all together, so that the semolina is well integrated (4 or 5 minutes). Allow to cool, and stir round once more, before putting it into a shallow bowl. Serve powdered with pistachio; cream is optional.

If you can do what my inspired Egyptian hostess did, and decorate the *Ma'Mounia* with fresh pomegranate seeds like little glittering rubies, you will find their sharpness relieves the rather cloying halva-ish sweetness of the *Ma'Mounia*.

Pain Louis XV

Although this is not strictly a Sunday Night Special, it is a typical French buffet standby, and looking back, I seem to recall it as an integral part of my life, when Eating for France. The chef at our French Embassy, in Berne (whose prodigal hand I have mentioned on p. 75), made this hollowed-out loaf, filled with the thinnest, almost transparent ham sandwiches, in the following manner:

Take two long sandwich loaves of day-old white bread – to hell with principles about natural flour. Cut the top off one, and set aside carefully, as it will become a lid to the finished product. With equal care scoop out all the bread inside the loaf leaving an empty shell, or case. The second loaf must now be cut into *very* thin, crustless, *well-buttered* slices. Fresh butter of course. Next place wafer-thin slices of ham between each piece, as for an ordinary sandwich. Cut in half, and then again, making four *small* pieces. Add mustard, chopped watercress or even pounded walnuts if you wish to be complicated. I prefer it plain; but the ham must be really good. Now pack all these fragile little square sandwiches back into the loaf, layer on layer. Replace the crusty top, or lid, and keep in a cool place until ready to serve.

It should not be made too long in advance or the loaf may harden, and the sandwiches curl at the edges. At all costs to liver or purse do not stint on the butter. There should be almost as much as ham!

In Memoriam: The East and West of the Romanian Table

When I lived in Bulgaria I sometimes borrowed or adapted the recipes of next-door countries, Romania and Yugoslavia and of course Turkey, to achieve a Balkan mish-mash, though Turkish cookery plays a dominant note in both lands and has a chapter to itself in these pages. Somehow, I never knew much of the Greek cuisine, for I did not know the country or its resources as I did the others. I was particularly fond of Romania's imaginative dishes. Here are some, simple or complicated. First, the basic *mamaliga*.

Mamaliga

1lb of cornmeal to 3 quarts of salted water. When the water boils furiously, rain in the corn meal, stirring constantly, till it slowly thickens: add a little hot water, if it has become too thick. Aim for the consistency of mashed potato. Turn out into a lightly greased cake-tin. It should cut like cake, according to some: personally, I prefer it more like the soft corn-meal mush of America's celebrated Southern cookery.

Mushrooms Baked in Sour Cream

Slice mushroom caps in half or, if big, in 3 slices, cover with sour cream, and top with *thin* slices of any mild cheese: bake in a slow oven. *Or:*

Mushrooms with Apples

Cut as above; stew very slowly in chicken stock, serve cold, with quarters of tart apples, and a sprinkle of paprika and parsley: good as an accompaniment to slices of smoked ham.

Ardei Umpluti

This is an elegant extra – the small pointed red or green paprika pods, slit open, stuffed with a mash of dark brown bread crumbs (or rice), salt and pepper and paprika (the strong kind), mixed with sour cream and a touch of vinegar, and some crushed walnuts and chips of garlic. I like plenty of that questionable substance added. Onions, instead, for the queasy.

Çiorba

Fish or chicken soup. *Çiorba* is the Turkish name for soup, and as a Turkish influence is felt throughout Balkan kitchens, the name sticks everywhere for a number of variations on the soupy theme. For this Romanian version, a simple fish soup has sour cream, yolk of egg and lemon juice beaten together as for a sauce, and added just before serving – when the soup is taken off the fire, of course, for fear of curdling. For basic fish soup make a stock of any slowly simmered white fish (not mackerel) with thinly-sliced onions, chopped dill and a tablespoonful of flour stirred with butter to thicken. One pound of fish to two quarts of water, with lemon added.

Pui cu Caise (Chicken with Apricots)

This is essentially an Arabic mélange, and once you have tried it, and liked it, I doubt you will ever wish to eat chicken without apricots. This is how the Romanian cooks did it, as a kind of stew. (You can also simply roast the chicken and add the apricots, to cook alongside, at half time. Dried apricots must be soaked in advance.) This is the Romanian way:

A plain roast chicken (or chicken pieces) is cooked in butter or oil. Dried apricots (soaked previously) are simmered in sugar and water, and slowly reduced to mushiness. Three medium-sized onions are fried lightly and also simmered in sugar and water. When they too are mushy, mix together the onions and apricots with some of the water in which the apricots were cooked. Add the chicken, or chicken pieces, sprinkle with brown sugar, add 2 teaspoons of lemon juice, salt and pepper. Put in a heavy pan and continue cooking, or rather simmering, for at least half an hour more. Stir occasionally to avoid sticking, and serve the chicken reposing on its apricot and onion bed.

Nedis Salad (good with a roast)

Smoked green peppers cut in rings (all skins, membranes and seeds removed), with chopped walnuts and a sharp vinegar dressing, and nasturtium seeds, crushed fine, sprinkled on top.

Sos de Mere

A typical Romanian sauce for veal, or poultry, is made of thin sliced tart apples, simmered in meat stock with a handful of fine-chopped parsley and brown sugar. When soft, place in blender, or push through coarse sieve. Add thick cream and one egg, well beaten, to the apple mush with plenty of salt and pepper. Simmer on low heat. Good with *cold* roast pork; a richer version of our classic apple sauce.

In the Balkans a pudding, or dessert, is generally referred to as *slatko*; this can mean a fruit compote, a tart, fritters or anything sweet. *Sutliash* is typically Bulgarian, but was often found in the simpler Romanian restaurants.

Bulgarian Sutliash

One cup of rice, turned till transparent, but not browned, in half a cup of walnut or grape-seed oil. Add a cup of sultanas, previously soaked in warm water; simmer the rice and sultana mixture in about 3 cups of water, or 4 of fruit juice. When the rice has become very soft, remove and sprinkle with white sugar. Serve cold in little bowls, one per person, with rose water or more fruit juice, or a powdering of cinnamon or almonds added.

Grand Food, Good Food
and Grub

You will find no recipes here for the three categories discussed in Chapter 13, p. 85. I would not care to attempt descriptions of the intricate convolutions of Grand Food in terms of the *haute cuisine*. Then Good Food is surely a matter of personal preference, one man's meat being another man's poison. As to Grub – homely, delightful Grub – we all know how to cook that ... don't we?

Nile-side Meals

Red Pottage (from Assiut)

This name has a nice Biblical ring, but there should be no 'exceeding bitter cry' to follow, as the Scriptures predicted, when they used the term Red Pottage to signify almost any manner of indulgence, gastronomic or otherwise.

Soak ½lb brown beans for 24 hours, then bring to the boil in fresh water to which a pinch of bicarbonate of soda and a generous knob of butter are added. At boiling point add 4 medium sized tomatoes, skinned and chopped coarsely, one beetroot, ditto, two or three onions, ditto, a piece of celery (optional), two lumps of brown sugar and a dessertspoonful of wine vinegar. Simmer for a couple of hours, sieve, or use the mixer to obtain a velvety texture, and serve with sour cream or yoghourt on the side. At Assiut it was without either; rather astringent, but good.

Foul Medammess (bean or lentil croquettes)

They are not complicated: first soak the beans, then stew slowly with chopped onion and parsley; drain away any water left. Form the bean mush into little sausagey shapes, and having rolled them in egg and bread crumbs, proceed to fry in oil, as with any other kind of croquette. Add such spices as you fancy – paprika, cumin, or coriander maybe, though as I am never tired of reminding you, it is often some purely local herb, or spice, or even the oil in which a dish is prepared that gives the true flavour, and remains tantalisingly aloof from our home kitchens, where we are left to approximate or invent, or 'cook till delicious'.

Macaroni Kom-Ombo

This is an Alexandrian way of transforming Mediterranean macaroni. However, I call it *macaroni Kom-Ombo* since I first ate it on one of those old-fashioned *dahabiyehs*, Nile house-boats now almost extinct. We were moored below the Crocodile Temple of Kôm-Ombo where once embalmed and sacred crocodiles would have cut one's appetite but now the macaroni won.

Chunks of thickish slices of unpeeled aubergine should be salted for a half hour, so that the bitter juices drain away. Press dry with a cloth. Dust lightly with flour, and fry in butter or oil, hardly allowing them to colour.

Cook the macaroni in the ordinary way. It should be the large, flat kind, the pieces about one inch long when cooked. In a buttered pie-dish place alternate layers of these macaroni pieces and the chunks of aubergine and pour over all a rather thick béchamel well flavoured with nutmeg (or it could be flavoured with cheese). Top with breadcrumbs, dot with butter, and heat through in a moderate oven till the top is browned. Simple, filling, and perfectly delicious.

Kounifa

This is a most ambitious pudding, and although I have watched it being made at the pastry-cook's, and heard it described lyrically, I shall not venture too far into the labyrinth of exactitudes. A rich, sweet, heavy batter is worked through tiny holes pierced in a hot metal plate until it resembles hair-fine threads of vermicelli. This is then fried in butter, and mixed with raisins and almonds, and sometimes cinnamon, till it solidifies into a *tarte renversée* – upside-down cake. It is then drenched in a honey sauce which I would sharpen with lemon. Not for dieters.

Muhallabieh

Another pudding, but particularly suited to fragile stomachs and the young: it is a staple, everyday dish all over Egypt. Boil up 1 quart of milk, add ½ breakfast cup water and a cup of ground rice. Keep stirring as it thickens. Add 1 small cup of sugar, 1 teaspoon orange or rose essence (but I think the rose is too sickly), continue stirring till it becomes the consistency of firm yoghourt. Add another dash of orange essence (*eau de fleurs d'oranger*) and serve icy cold, in little individual bowls. If sprinkled classically with chopped pistachio nuts or grated orange peel it seems less insipid or nurseryish.

The Hubbard Cupboard
Emergency Dishes from Small Nothings

For a quick undemanding soup, try *Aïgou Boulido*, described in 'Village Inventions' (p. 130).

For the 'kind of' kedgeree that can be made from the ingredients mentioned earlier, proceed as follows:

Cook rice in usual way, hard-boil the eggs, and put the anchovy fillets to soak (10 minutes) to remove the excess saltiness. When rice is ready, drain, add the eggs, coarsely chopped, likewise the parsley, then add small snippets of anchovy. Failing the anchovies a large spoonful of anchovy essence must do, to flavour and faintly colour the rice. Or saffron, or tomato purée. Stir in a generous knob of butter, and serve on blazing hot toast, or fried bread triangles. Agreeable as this can be, do not call it kedgeree – just call it savoury rice.

Here is another rice standby. A *kind of* pilaff:

Put a handful of dried raisins or sultanas to soak in warm water, also some dried mushrooms (if your cupboard yields these helpful adjuncts). If not, make out with onions only, sliced fine and simmered in oil. Even if you can only round up one last, withered rasher of bacon, it will help; fry it up with the rest, and when rather overcooked, cut into small pieces. As soon as the rice is ready and drained, stir in the onions, mushrooms, raisins and the bits of bacon; add the oil or butter in which these ingredients were cooked, and fork lightly. Then, sprinkle with grated orange peel or powdered cinnamon, as they do in Armenian kitchens. This follows the general lines I have described for an Armenian pilaff on p. 153 and I think it could well go by that name.

A propos rice, Italian cooks sometimes make the most of a plain rice by adding red wine while the rice is cooking. It gives a faint, faraway vinous aroma, and colours the rice a delicate beigey-pink.

If you are in such dire straits that you have none of the foregoing scraps, but can round up some polenta (maize flour), a packet of which should be in every store cupboard beside the rice, then with some of those ignoble-looking scraps of cheese which always seem to be lying around, you can produce a cheese *mamaliga* much as Romanians do, for in that country polenta is cherished, *mamaliga* ranking as a national dish. See p. 157.

Here are some potato stand-bys, to be tried out according to your resources.

Champ (an Irish potato and leek speciality)

Two pounds, more or less, of hot mashed potatoes mixed with several fine-chopped leeks and spring onions cooked in milk. Drain, and beat all together till a pale green mixture is obtained. Make a hole in the centre and pour in as much melted butter as possible. The more the better. A large spoonful of butter goes with each helping of *champ*.

Latké (Jewish potato cakes)

Six medium potatoes are peeled and grated and set aside to drain. Four tablespoons of grated onion are then added. Two tablespoons of white flour are mixed with two large beaten eggs and a little salt, added to the potato and onion mixture. About six tablespoons of corn oil, for choice, are heated to smoking point. Spoonfuls of the potato mixture are then dropped in to brown on both sides. The heat should now be lowered a little, so that the raw potato mixture cooks thoroughly. The *latké* cakes should be well done after 6 minutes a side. Serve with the gravy from a roast; if not, perhaps in a mustard and tomato sauce, though this is not usual. In Prague they gave me mushroom sauce with the *latké*. I had begun the meal with a cold vinegary *bortsch*, and ended with cheese *blintzes*. It was a thoroughly traditional Jewish meal, a proper prelude to *The Dybbuk*.

Kufleta Kartofi (Bulgarian dumplings)

Cook two pounds of peeled potatoes (floury ones, if obtainable: they seem hard to find now). Mash with a little milk. Add about 6 dessertspoons of breadcrumbs, brown for choice, at least 3 table-spoons of chopped parsley, salt and pepper to taste and, having rolled the mixture into round, or sausagey shaped pieces, fry in plenty of oil: *not* olive oil – grape-seed oil or corn oil is best here. Dill pickle sauce is good with this. Mince one onion small, fry in oil, add a little flour and continue cooking. Then add a cup of consommé, chicken or beef cubes are all right, with four or five dill pickles diced small and a tablespoon of parsley. Heat and allow to simmer for 10 minutes or so. A teaspoon of sugar before serving is optional. Some stir in sour cream at the last moment, that again is optional.

Kugelis (Russian potato pudding)

Grate two pounds of peeled potatoes, rather coarsely, add salt and 2 small eggs or 1 large one. Mix all together and put into an oven-proof dish into which you have poured about 4 or 5 tablespoons of melted butter, or butter and oil, half and half or, if you have it, clarified butter. Bake uncovered till the potatoes are crisp and brown – about 30 minutes medium heat. Now turn the pan upside down on a large plate and ease the mixture out of the dish. It will have a lovely crisp golden-brown crust. Turn the whole thing over again, and replace it in the baking dish, so that the brown top is now at the bottom. Return to the oven and leave it there till the less cooked part is also a golden-brown crust. Serve it on a well-heated, flat dish with more melted butter as sauce. Slivers of fried onion rings are sometimes sprinkled over before serving the *kugelis*, which by its topsy-turvy cooking recalls the Persian *kateh* or rice *renversé*, also with a golden crust.

Last-minute Puddings

For emergency puddings, a mix-up of stale sweet biscuits is a good start. Butter a pie-dish, and crumble in a layer of biscuits. Spread this with jam, add more biscuit crumbs, and more jam, in layers. The last layer should be biscuit crumbs, dotted with butter. Brown in the oven and serve with a sauce made from a spoonful or two of jam, thinned with lemon juice, and almost any alcohol to hand, rum, cognac. . .?

A variation of this can be made from any stale plain cake – preferably ginger. Cut in slices, and spread marmalade between each slice and tie it round like a parcel to prevent it falling apart. Heat through and serve with a sauce, as above. Don't forget to remove the string.

The boring banana is one of those left-over objects that tend to lie about, blackening fast. But bananas are transformed, if peeled, split in half lengthwise, and arranged side by side, in a fire-proof dish. They must be soused in lemon juice and or alcohol (not whisky). Rum or cognac are the best. A lot of sugar should be added before heating the dolled-up bananas under the grill, or in a slow oven. They should be served in the same dish, for they collapse if pushed around.

If you only have two little cream cheeses left, and you are four at table, beat up the cheese with a little yoghourt (the unflavoured kind, of course, you are never without *that*). Then mix in some instant coffee grains and sugar, and pile this suave mixture into little ramekins, one per person. Don't neglect to dust a very little powdered coffee on top, as a last touch. It will begin to melt, and form decorative dark streaks on the pale *café au lait* coloured base. If you have some plain chocolate, try grating chips of it over the cream in place of the coffee grounds.

And if you find the foregoing recipes too bleak, then take care that your larder cupboard does not leave you in the lurch.

Arabian Aromas

Kebash-el-Attarine (a superb Arabian dish)

This is for those who like exotic aromas carried to extremes. A leg of lamb is spit-roasted, for preference, though the oven will do. After being carved into thick portions, fat *and* lean, the pieces are dredged with powdered pistachio nuts, and then smothered in melted honey to which pounded almonds have been added. Traditionally, the whole is served up on a bed of puréed apricots. Feeling faint? Then bring yourself round with the following sharp salad.

Munkazina

This is of Moroccan origin, though I have eaten it all across North Africa. Slices of peeled oranges – well peeled, no pith – are combined with a scattering of thinly sliced onions and black olives. As dressing, oil and vinegar with salt, pepper and paprika, to which I add a pinch of brown sugar.

Pickles

These are an addition to the Arab table and always seem to me unreasonably popular in lands where more subtle flavours flourish. I associate pickles with those depressing cold cuts often served up with left-overs on Western tables, along with beetroot slices awash in vinegar. The pickles Middle Eastern households make, or buy from those decorative street-booths that specialise in them, are arranged in large bottles, bright pink, crimson, yellow or green, a whole vegetable kingdom of imprisoned cauliflowerets, onions, turnips, cucumber or green peppers, floating in spiced vinegar. But since pickles are easily obtainable from any good grocer, I shall opt out of attempting to encourage home-pickling.

Hummus bi Taheeni (a rich creamy sauce, or dip)

Two cups of chick-peas are soaked in slightly salted water. Drain and simmer in fresh water till soft, perhaps 2 hours. Remove from the heat, cool slightly then add drop by drop, 1 cup of sesame or taheena oil and 1 cup of lemon juice, a strong pinch of cumin and one of paprika. When a thick paste is obtained, add at least 2 cloves of crushed garlic; if the paste remains too thick, thin carefully with a little cold water. Serve in a shallow bowl, garnished with parsley. A variation of this can be made with beans, or lentils, in place of the chick peas, in which case it is called *foul bi taheeni*.

Baba Ganoush (aubergine purée with sesame oil)

Put 2lbs of plump aubergines in the oven. Remove when the interior seems soft (test with a fork). Scoop out the flesh and mash, adding 4 or 5 cloves of garlic crushed fine. Add 1 cup of sesame oil and $\frac{1}{2}$ cup of lemon juice. Put the mixture through the blender. When a homogeneous mass is obtained, fork in some coarse-chopped parsley, which will give the mixture a grainy texture.

Such purées call for Arab bread, or any *pitta* loaf obtainable. There are now a number of such excellent prepared loaves on the market. Adding sesame seeds, thickly spread over the top of a white loaf which has been brushed with sesame oil, before re-heating in the oven, might go well enough with a number of Arab *mezas*. Oddly, those brittle flat biscuits of Jewish tradition, called *matzos*, are also good with *mezas*, perhaps because geographically they are neighbours. *Flat-bröd*, crisp rye biscuits from Scandinavia, which should, in theory, be as good, are oddly out of key.

Kibbeh (a Lebanese speciality)

Small chunks of lamb and onion are pounded, or put through the blender, till of a thick paste consistency. Mix together with *burghul* (obtainable in packets) to which a *very* little water is added. (Specialists use ice-water, which is supposed to keep the mixture extra smooth.) Some cooks add finely ground parsley. Salt and pepper, of course. There are numerous ways of cooking the *kibbeh* once the preliminary pounding is done. One way is to put a layer of *kibbeh* in a flat greased casserole, then put a layer of chopped onions, *coarse* ground meat, pine nuts and cinnamon, all fried brown together. Follow with another layer of the original *kibbeh*, and end with the onion and meat mixture. Dab with butter, or pour melted or clarified butter (*samna*) over all, and cook in a moderate oven for about half an hour.

Samna

Here, a note on clarified butter, which is used almost exclusively in Arab cooking, and is known as *ghee* in Indian kitchens. It is made by melting butter in a bain-marie and straining it through thin muslin. It goes a long way and has the merit of never 'catching' or turning brown over a high flame, in the way which butter can ruin a delicate sauce. For myself, I cook almost entirely in corn oil, or add a minimum of butter. Olive oil I reserve for salads, or specific recipes where it is essential.

Golden Rice

Since rice is much used to accompany fish (though I shall always prefer the faithful spud of my London childhood), I suggest the following as a good base on which to serve most fish – especially a white fish. This is how it was prepared at sunset on the beach at Aqaba, Jordan's small and sole port beside the Sinai peninsula, where the fish almost leapt out of the water onto one's plate. Prepare the rice any way which has proved most successful, and to obtain a golden colour, add a pinch of saffron or turmeric powder and some fresh ground pepper to the water in which the rice is cooking. To obtain a salmony pink hue, add 3 tablespoons of tomato purée (yes, even from a tin). But remember, the amount of these flavourings and the strength of the colouring they impart must be adjusted to the amount of rice being prepared. For certain fish dishes the accompanying rice is sprinkled over with curlicues of fried onion, or pine nuts. In very grand Arab establishments, such as the Caliph Hārūn-al-Rashid's, rice dishes were sometimes powdered with gold-dust – if we are to believe *The Arabian Nights' Entertainments*. And why shouldn't we? In some ancient streets of the East it still reads like accounts of everyday life.

Coffee

The basic difference between Turkish and Arabic coffee is that Turkish coffee is made rapidly, in small quantities. Boiling water is thrown onto the fine ground coffee, heated up, and served as a rich sugary brew. But Arabic coffee is cooked, stewed, if you like, unsweetened, for as long as you like, the coffee being kept simmering in a large pot. This gives it an astringent transparency.

Arabic Coffee for Four (a simplified version)

This must be Mocha beans and green cardamom seeds roasted together to become a light brown – no more: then *ground* not pulverised, into a grain resembling in size fine Nescafé grains. For 1 litre of boiling water (this coffee being made in quantity, unlike the Turkish), add 6 tablespoons of the grains, and a sprinkle of saffron or cardamom seeds. It is best to use a lidded pot or kettle, so that the water does not reduce too much as it simmers. After at least half an hour or more, filter the liquid into another pot, and then the brew will be clear, strong and slightly bitter. A *little* sugar added, if you must – but this is not usual for so virile a drink.

Turkish Coffee for Four

4 teaspoons of sugar, if you serve it '*orta*' or '*mazbout*' (medium sweet), 4 heaped teaspoons of coffee, 4 coffee cups of water, though this depends on the size of your cups. Let us assume you have the standard, small after-dinner kind.

Put sugar and water into the *ibrik*, or *jezve*, a long-handled brass pot essential for Turkish coffee, and easily obtainable. Bring to the boil, stirring until the sugar is completely dissolved. Stir in the coffee, and bring up to the boil again. When the froth rises to the top dangerously, snatch the pot off the flame, and allow the froth to subside. Then return to the flame and heat up again. Repeat this manœuvre three times. Add a dash of cold water, after the last rising; this settles the grounds, without disturbing the creamy froth or *kaïmak* that marks properly made coffee. Serve at once, without stirring, and do not allow your guests any spoons, so that they are not tempted to disturb the sediment which lies at the bottom of the cup. To be very voluptuous, add a few drops of rose essence.

Mint Tea (a less cloying version than generally made)

Brew a strong infusion of green tea, half and half with a good Indian brand (the latter must not be too fiercely strong, like the British cuppa).

Add some crushed mint leaves, fresh, not dried, and leave standing for a few minutes to gather fragrance.

Then throw away half, and pour freshly boiled water over the remainder. Stir, and serve immediately, in small glasses. A spoon standing up in the glass will prevent it cracking from the heat; beside it, a sprig of mint for elegance. Classically, sugar is added, the amount is a matter of preference. In some cafés the mint is replaced by a sprig of verbena.

And I must pray my Moroccan friends to forgive me the heresy of my adaptation.

A Note on Yoghourt

Throughout the pages of this book, and particularly in any of those chapters dwelling on the food of the Middle East and thereabouts, one huge span of similarity is apparent. Across North Africa to the Persian Gulf, by way of Turkey, Syria, Greece and the Balkans, all these many races and cultures are united in one common gastronomic factor or ingredient – Yoghourt. It goes by a number of different names. In the Arab world it is called Laban; in the Caucasus, Matsun; in Turkey and the Balkans Yogurtlu, the 'g' not being sounded; thus, if you wish to be correct, pronounce it Yahoutlu. In Iran, it is called Mast, and diluted with water, becomes Abdug, a cooling drink. It is also used there to tenderise meat, and as I myself have proved, is a sovereign remedy for sun-burn.

Those who do not care for this miraculous substance, which is both health-giving and delicious, need not read on. But for the enthusiasts, a word of advice. Do not imagine that the commercial brands of yoghourt which now flood the Western market bear much likeness to the real stuff. (I do not bother to mention those sugary, fruity yoghourts which are nursery puddings.) The best yoghourt is made from sheep or buffalo milk – the cow has no place here and goats' milk is rather rank. The supreme vintage kind is only obtained where there are either of those useful animals, the sheep or the black buffalo – their yoghourt being of a *clotted* richness. I have found that I can achieve a passable imitation by mixing the best commercial natural yoghourt (unsweetened) with one third of cottage cheese, and some sour cream, to taste. If you wish to cook with yoghourt, be careful to add a little flour, otherwise it disintegrates in the heat. Add a coffee spoon of flour, cornflour or white of egg.

There are many recipes for making yoghourt, and all sorts of set-ups of little pots, and cultures to start things going, so I shall not expand on how to make it at home. The problem of making it oneself is largely a question of maintaining a steady temperature while it germinates.

In my Bulgarian kitchen Raïna, my Macedonian cook, kept each batch snug beside the stove wrapped in one of her old flannel petticoats.

The Kitchen Chemist

For bee or wasp stings a vinegar poultice or an application of ammonia.
For cuts – of a superficial kind – a temporary disinfectant of brandy or vodka.
For burns – superficial again – an ice cube, held on the burn, or immersion in cold water or an application of sliced raw onion. An old country recipe suggests a piece of cotton, saturated with treacle! The principle, anyway, is to keep air away from the burn to avoid blistering.
For suspected poisoning the whites of five or six eggs, to be drunk immediately, is said to neutralise the evil.

For tired eyes compresses of cold tea (without milk or sugar, of course).
For sunburn yoghourt (unsweetened kind) smothered all over the afflicted areas and left on till morning if possible. Yoghourt also makes a base or foundation lotion, smoothed carefully over a baked face, if social life demands an appearance.
To remove make-up olive oil or any vegetable oil – which also nourishes.
To refresh a fast raddling face sliced cucumber or flat champagne.
For a setting lotion beer, or light ale: it dries quicker than water.

For rheumatic joints or sprains a raw cabbage leaf poultice left on overnight.
For a bad cold mustard plasters or a hot mustard bath and or onion porridge.
For a disturbed stomach a bicarbonate of soda and lemon drink; chips of garlic (which disinfect).
For a tired liver artichokes, *ad lib*, and the water in which they are cooked.

The trots – If you are travelling or eating in the exotic way, alas, you are liable to disturbances. Thus I am offering you a cure which has saved many of my friends – raw green apples, peeled and grated and *nothing else* for twenty-four hours except very weak tea without milk or sugar. This strange-seeming cure has worked for me for over forty years, since it was given to me by an aged Polish doctor encountered on one of my excursions along wilder shores.

For a good night's sleep a glass of hot red wine spiced with cloves. Teetotallers might do well enough with hot milk and honey. (Better of course with whisky added.) There are innumerable *tisanes* on the market which are considered soporifics, as well as digestives. Personally I find them wishy-washy deceptions, but the French take them ritually – particularly for the sake of their digestions.

Short Index of Recipes